5/4/2002

To Aven[...]

^ inspiration to visit these places in
the next fifty years!

With love

Chris & Donald

SCOTLAND
THE WILD PLACES

To the eyes of the man of imagination, nature is imagination itself. As a man is so he sees.
William Blake 1757–1827

SCOTLAND
THE WILD PLACES

TEXT AND PHOTOGRAPHS BY COLIN PRIOR

CONSTABLE • LONDON

FIRST PUBLISHED IN THE UK IN 2001 BY CONSTABLE.
AN IMPRINT OF CONSTABLE & ROBINSON LTD

CONSTABLE & ROBINSON
3 THE LANCHESTERS
162 FULHAM PALACE ROAD
LONDON W6 9ER
WWW.CONSTABLEROBINSON.COM

A COPY OF THE BRITISH LIBRARY CATALOGUING IN
PUBLICATION DATA IS AVAILABLE FROM THE BRITISH LIBRARY.

ISBN 1-84119-315-1

SGURR NAN GILLEAN FROM MARSCO, CLOUD INVERSION, CUILLINS, ISLE OF SKYE

Contents

Introduction

The Scottish landscape is unique. There can be few places in the developed world where the absence of humanity from the land seems so acute. Large areas of the Highlands stand in remote isolation, dominated by mountain ranges and sea lochs. As most of the land is unsuitable for agriculture, sheep-farming and stalking are the main activities, with tourism as the principle source of income. For many people – including myself – the appeal of rural Scotland is not what is there but rather what is not. The Highlands offer unparalleled ease of access to wild and remote locations: mountains to climb, beaches to walk on and watch the weather go by, places shielded by distance from the tide of commercialism. Wild places like these take us back to our roots and help us escape the intensity of modern life. In the words of the American writer and environmentalist, Wallace Stegner, writing in *The Wilderness Letter* (1960), 'We simply need that wild country available to us, even if we never do more than drive to its edges and look in. For it can be a means of reassuring ourselves of our sanity as creatures, a part of the geography of hope.'

The Scottish Highlands are the domain of the mountaineer. With 277 mountains over 3000ft (914m) – the Munros – there are endless challenges for those seeking adventure. The most rewarding season for climbing is winter, when low temperatures create superb visibility and clarity. To linger on a summit late on a winter's day and watch the sun go down is an unforgettable experience which helps put life into perspective.

Glaciation during the last ice age was responsible for shaping many of the natural features we recognize in the Scottish landscape today. Glencoe is a good example of this, with arête-type peaks, deep scalloped corries, 'V' shaped glens and the ribbon lakes of Lochan na h'Achalaise and Loch Ba on Rannoch Moor. Glacial action also produced deep sea lochs such as Loch Hourn and Loch Nevis, which flooded as the ice receded. The region of Torridon in the north-west is probably one of the best areas to observe the effects of glacial erosion, portraying all the classic features of a landscape shaped by ice.

The humid Atlantic atmosphere gives the Highlands a variety and subtlety of colour that is absent from sunnier countries. Rain, mist and clouds sustain the vegetation which produces the seasonal tapestries of colour. While the Alps and the Himalayas are known for their magnitude and scale, the Scottish mountains are enigmatic and elegant and are seen in constantly changing patterns of light.

At one time Scotland was heavily wooded with birch, rowan and Scots pine. The Wood of Caledon formerly extended from Glen Coe to Braemar and from Glen Lyon to Glen Affric. Harbouring bear, wild boar and wolf, the ancient forest was systematically destroyed: the trees were felled and burned by warring clans and later, in the seventeenth century, supplied fuel and timber for iron-smelting and shipbuilding. Recent initiatives by Scottish Natural Heritage to re-establish the original forest have been extremely encouraging. Native trees have been re-planted and the enclosure of areas by fencing has prevented sheep and red deer from grazing on the saplings. As the natural vegetation returns, so do the birds, with great spotted woodpecker, willow warbler, greenfinch and sparrowhawk returning to their familiar habitat.

My own interest in mountains goes back to my childhood, when I developed a passion for the natural world. Wild landscapes, birds and animals captured my imagination in a way that nothing else did. As my fascination grew I searched for ways to express the enjoyment I felt in wild places. I was in my early twenties when I began to experiment with photography as the medium through which I could share my most deeply felt visual experiences. Ironically, my first published photographs were not of mountains but of underwater landscapes. Having spent an apprenticeship photographing the fauna of the Scottish sea lochs, I travelled overseas to record the splendour of coral reefs in the Red Sea, Indian Ocean and Caribbean. It was a challenging time, but I needed more. I wanted to make bigger visual statements about the natural world – images that could communicate with people at a subconscious level, appealing to their psyche as the wild and remote places I loved did to my own.

In 1989 I bought my first panoramic camera. Designed and manufactured in Munich by Linhof, it was fitted with the excellent Schneider Super-Angulon 90mm f5.6 lens and produced 6 x 17 panoramic images from roll film. The 3:1 image ratio was superb and the impact it produced could

7

convey something of the excitement of the original visual experience. This was the aesthetic for which I had searched for so long and I knew that, if I combined it with my personal feelings about the natural world, the results could be very special. I set about producing a portfolio of the Scottish Highlands and Islands with the specific intention of publishing a book. *Highland Wilderness*, featuring my first Scottish collection of panoramic work, was published in 1993, but I felt that there was much more to do and began work on a second portfolio. The result – this book – is intended to be a celebration of the enduring natural heritage of Scotland, exploring its relationship with the elements through the seasons.

Seasonal light

Most of my images are planned rather than spontaneous: my philosophy is to visit an area first to establish the optimum location and time for photography. The geography will dictate whether the image will be shot at sunrise or sunset, and in which season. I find it desirable to shoot during the 'magic hours' (the hour which precedes dusk and the hour after dawn) when the sun is low in the sky and produces a warmer light.

Some people imagine, when I talk about taking photographs at sunrise or sunset, that my intention is to photograph a large red ball rising or falling in the sky. It is of course quite the reverse: I usually want the sun at my back in order to use its warm rays to illuminate the landscape. The season is also important as it will ultimately dictate the position of the sun at sunrise and sunset – the sun's movement during the year affects not only the amount but also the direction and angle of the light reaching the landscape. For images that include the sea, a knowledge of high and low water times is desirable.

The challenge facing the landscape photographer is to be in the right place at the right time. Previsualization directs me to events I plan to witness, to capture those rare moments when light and land come together. The same technique was used by our early hunting ancestors, who had not only to pre-visualize where game might appear but also where to conceal themselves to guarantee success in a situation which had not yet developed. Even a polar bear knows better than just to sit down and wait for its prey to arrive.

My favourite season for photography in Scotland is from late autumn – towards the end of October – through the winter months until late March. With the onset of spring in early May, an explosion of new growth creates a vibrancy of fresh green foliage and is another exciting period to record. Ironically, it is the late summer months of July and August that are least appealing: while the weather is generally stable, the landscape and foliage present a tonal monotony of green, with little contrast or visual impact. It is during this period that I concentrate on seascapes, making use of beaches and rock, vibrant sea colours and skies to create powerful images.

This book has been structured to reflect the changing seasons. Instead of categorizing the images

by region or mountain group, the four chapters are divided by the equinoxes and solstices. Each chapter contains all the photographs taken between two of these celestial events. This seasonal categorization is particularly relevant to my photographs, which depend largely on the changing position of sunrise and sunset at different times of the year and on optimum weather conditions. The portfolio in each chapter portrays a distinct seasonal synergy.

The sun's ecliptic

The equinoxes and solstices, which serve as markers in the celestial calendar, indirectly affect all of us, and it is intriguing to observe how the mechanics of these phenomena impact on every aspect of the natural world during the cycle of the year. The earth's annual orbit around the sun takes 365.25 days, a day being the time taken by the earth to spin once on its axis. On earth, we perceive this orbit as the sun moving along an imaginary line called the ecliptic. The earth and most of the planets orbit the sun in more or less the same plane, so that the planets appear to stay fairly close to the ecliptic, against a background of stars. Ancient astronomers attached great importance to the band of constellations visible along the ecliptic, and it is these which are collectively known as the zodiac.

Seasonal changes occur because the earth's axis of rotation is tilted at 23.5 degrees to the plane of its orbit around the sun. As the sun's position in relation to the earth appears to travel along the ecliptic, it appears to be above the equator for one half of the year, producing the northern summer, and below the equator for the other half (northern winter), thus crossing the equator twice in a year.

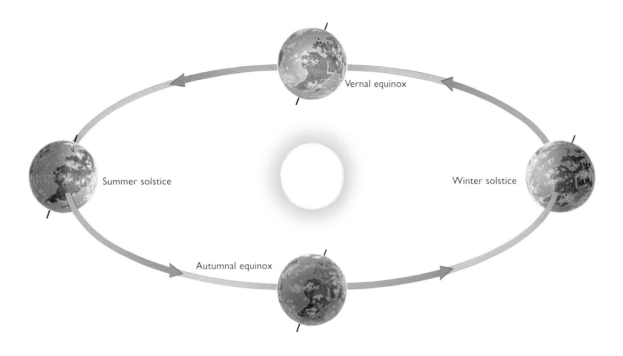

Vernal equinox

Summer solstice

Winter solstice

Autumnal equinox

10

The equinoxes

At the times when the sun's ecliptic is crossing the plane of the equator, day and night are of nearly equal length, so these dates are called the equinoxes (from the Latin for 'equal night'). In the northern hemisphere, the vernal or spring equinox occurs in March, as the sun is moving northwards along the ecliptic. The autumnal equinox occurs in September, as the sun is moving southwards. The precise times of the equinoxes vary: they occur about six hours later each year, until they jump backwards by about eighteen hours in a leap year. It is only after a complete leap-year cycle of four centuries that the dates and times will be repeated exactly. In the last century the times of the equinoxes ranged between the latest dates – 21 March at 7 p.m. and 24 September at 6 a.m. in 1903 – to the earliest, 20 March at 8 a.m. and 22 September at 5 p.m. in 2000.

The orbit of the earth around the sun is not a circle but an ellipse. The effect of this is that the earth moves fastest when it is closest to the sun (around 3 January) and slowest when it is furthest away (around 4 July). This unequal motion causes variations in the length of the solar day and in the times of sunrise and sunset, so that the sun is not at its highest point at precisely local noon each day. The difference between noon as measured by a clock and the moment when the sun crosses the meridian is called the 'equation of time', and the adjustment needed to match the two can be as much as sixteen minutes in either direction.

The solstices

Midway between the equinoxes come the solstices, when the sun is at its furthest from the celestial equator (the projection of the earth's equator onto the sky). The summer solstice occurs around 21 June, and the winter solstice around 21 December, with the precise dates and times varying throughout the same 400-year cycle as for the equinoxes.

In the northern hemisphere, the winter solstice is the time when the sun reaches its southernmost distance from the celestial equator. It is the day on which the sun appears lowest in the sky at noon and is the shortest day of the year. Oddly, however, the time of sunrise continues to get later after the solstice. This anomaly arises because, close to the winter solstice, the equation of time is changing at its fastest. During the period between 16 December and 5 January, the time at which the sun crosses the meridian varies by ten minutes, and this is reflected in the times of sunrise and sunset, as measured by the clock. During the same period, the sun's height in the sky and the day length are changing very slowly, so that the rapid change in the equation of time outpaces the slow change in day length.

While the equinoxes and solstices provide precise dates for the beginning of each season, they do not exactly correspond with the regular climatic changes which prompt the seasonal transformation of the landscape. The earth responds gradually to the change in energy it receives from the sun, and the warming and cooling of the atmosphere and oceans occur over several weeks, while many other factors influence local climatic patterns. An accurate measure of the direction and angle of the sun is, however, of paramount importance to the photographer.

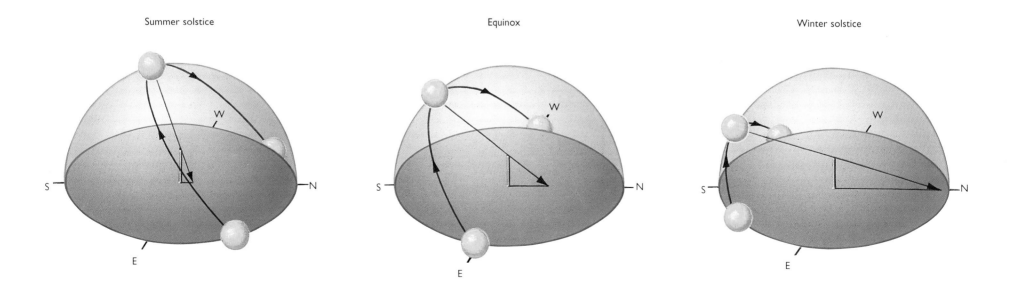

Summer solstice   Equinox   Winter solstice

PATH OF THE SUN ACROSS THE SKY AT DIFFERENT TIMES OF THE YEAR AS VIEWED FROM SCOTLAND

Vernal Equinox
to Summer Solstice

Of the four seasonal markers of the year, the vernal equinox probably has the greatest impact on our lives. For those living through the Scottish winter, in what at times seems like perpetual gloom, the lengthening hours of daylight are always welcomed with enthusiasm. The increased light and temperature trigger nature's annual renewal, as the sap rises and the trees are dressed in a veil of fresh green. Catkins of hazel and willow signal regeneration and herald the new season.

Gorse explodes into a profusion of yellow, and linnet and stonechat perch amongst its flowers to broadcast their territories. In the river estuaries, crooning eider drakes, with their distinctive black and white plumage, follow the ebb and flow of the tide. Eiders build their nests close to the high tide line. In late May the duck plucks down from her breast to line the nest and lays from four to six light green eggs.

In the mountains, spring moves at a slower pace, and winter retains its grip on the summits. Low temperatures, intensified by altitude, often maintain alpine conditions into May, with little perceptible change. The raven, however, is not dissuaded from breeding and is one of the first birds to do so, nesting on high rock faces from mid-February.

Bounded by the sea lochs of Hourn and Nevis, the peninsula of Knoydart embodies some of the finest mountain scenery in Scotland (*pages 44–45*). Enigmatic and remote, its three Munros – Ladhar Bheinn, 3346ft (1020m), Luinne Bheinn, 3081ft (939m), and Meall Buidhe, 3104ft (946m) – rise from extremely rough and rocky corries and are separated by the high pass of the Mam Barrisdale. Access is principally by a long walk from Kinloch Hourn along the south shore of Loch Hourn to Barrisdale, or by boat from Mallaig or Arnisdale. Wildlife is abundant on the peninsula, with a wide variety of species including otter, golden eagle, peregrine falcon, seal and red-throated diver.

Knoydart is the quintessential Scottish landscape, with glaciated mountains rising from deeply indented sea lochs. For me, it is this blend of mountain and marine environments, with its variety of associated wildlife, which makes the area so appealing (*pages 18–19*). Over the years, I have made many trips into Knoydart, each of them in its own way unique. I recall my first excursion in early spring, when snow lay deep along the path from Kinloch Hourn to Barrisdale and we struggled under the weight of our packs, laden with camping and photographic equipment.

As we passed stands of old Scots pine, we encountered red deer feeding close to the footpath. Such was their hunger that they took little account of us and continued to forage as we approached. This was my closest encounter with wild deer and, in a strange way, it helped me to feel part of this formidable environment. In their apparent acceptance of our presence, perhaps these wild beasts perceived that we were after all confronted by the same adversity and faced the same immediate problems as they did: we too needed to find shelter, food and warmth. Suddenly, to my urbanized mind, came a real awareness of the sheer effort and hardship it would take to sustain life in such a wild place. Writing for *Time* magazine, Roger Rosenblatt wrote: 'Nature is undemocratic: in the wilds, wet or dry, the individual has no dignity. The strong eat the weak, and all one's humanistic ideals of equality and justice are drowned out in acts of casual murder.'

Despite the effort involved, the beginning of the year offers excellent potential for mountain photography as the sun is beginning to rise further north, illuminating many of the north-facing slopes at dawn. Mindful of this, I planned to photograph Lochnagar and its great north-east corrie at this season. I had made two previous trips from Glen Muick, climbing onto Meikle Pap, 3215ft (980m), for dawn, to discover that in early January the sun illuminated the north-east corrie only momentarily. It then slid behind the south side of the mountain where it remained for the rest of the day. I concluded two

things: first, that I was in the wrong location and, second, that I needed to shoot the mountain later in the year, when the sun rose yet further north, ensuring that sufficient light illuminated the corrie at dawn. Two years passed before the right conditions prevailed, by which time I had explored the surrounding area and established my new location. I shot the final image in early April at around 7.10 a.m. (*pages 34–35*).

I had planned to photograph the Sound of Luing in Argyll during the month of June. South-east of Mull, the area known as Nether Lorn includes the islands of Seil, Luing, Scarba, and the Isles of the Sea. The narrow straits between the islands give rise to notorious tide-races, notably the Grey Dog and the Corryvreckan to the north and south of Scarba, the Fladda Narrows at the Sound of Luing and the Dorus Mor off Craignish Point. Having studied the map and previously photographed from Seil and Luing, I concluded that the ultimate viewpoint in the area would be from the highest point on Scarba. I made contact with a lobster fisherman based in Luing who agreed to ferry me out to this uninhabited island. It was a beautiful day and I set off with a full rucksack, planning to camp overnight on the summit to shoot both at dusk and dawn. The walk over rough moorland was strenuous and, as I neared the summit, I caught sight of a golden eagle as it rose from a rock and sailed silently away.

As I arrived on the summit, the entire view became visible and it was awesome – the Garvellachs lay before me: Ben More, 3169ft (966m), the most westerly Munro on Mull, lay behind; to the east were the islands of Lunga, Belnahua, Fladda, Seil and Luing. To the north lay Loch Linnie and Fort William with Ben Nevis, 4409ft (1344m), and the Grey Corries. Further east, Loch Melfort and the distinctive outline of Ben Cruachan, 3694ft (1126m), were all clearly visible. The panorama was breathtaking. Quickly I made a survey of the high points and established a location for photography, pitched my one-man tent, made supper and waited for the sun to drop. With the tide at full ebb, the ensuing sunset was spectacular and I sought to capture the spirit of the place in the warm evening light (*pages 46–47*).

The following morning the sun dawned at just after 5 a.m. and I headed back over the top to photograph Jura to the south-west. As I waited for the sun to climb higher in the sky I marvelled at the Gulf of Corryvrekan, where legends tell that the local inhabitants once lured marauding Norsemen to their deaths in its whirlpool – the most powerful in western Europe (*pages 26–27*). Then I noticed a couple of feathers on the ground near my feet. On closer inspection they turned out to be the feathers of a golden eagle, both primary and secondary wing feathers and a breast

14

feather, shed at the eagle's preening stone. The bird had instinctively selected this spot – as I had – for its strategic location, commanding an almost 360-degree view of the surrounding islands.

The discovery of the feathers suddenly gave me a fresh insight – the contrast of microcosm and macrocosm created for me a unique perspective on the landscape. I now surveyed it as if I too were an eagle, the master of this magnificent environment, with the freedom of the air and the ability to cross water to reach other islands, and it was a strange sensation. Finding the eagle's feathers seemed as powerful an experience as discovering the landscape – or perhaps each was compounded by the other.

A'Mhaighdean ('the Maiden'), 3173ft (967m), is Britain's remotest mountain, standing at the head of Fionn Loch in the Fisherfield Forest in Wester Ross. Previous trips to the surrounding mountains had convinced me that it would offer superb potential for panoramic photography. Accompanied by my father, I set off from the Dundonnell Hotel on 20 June, just before the summer solstice, and walked to the Shenavall Bothy, which sits beneath the 2986ft (910m) peak of Beinn Dearg Mor (*pages 30–31*). Here we spent the first night in a rather midge-infested room. The following morning we departed for A'Mhaighdean, carrying full rucksacks with tent, sleeping bags, mats, food, drinks, cameras and tripod, to ford the two rivers the path crosses. In spring the icy meltwaters of the Abhainn Loch an Nid and the Abhainn Gleann na Muice can create a formidable barrier, which sharply focuses the mind.

The path climbs steeply up to Fuar Loch Mor, lying in a corrie between Ruadh Stac Mor, 3012ft (918m), and A'Mhaighdean, and its cool waters were a welcome relief in the baking sun. On reaching the bealach, we set up camp and continued up the north-east ridge to the summit with camera equipment only. We reached the summit at 7.45 p.m. and were confronted with a truly spectacular view. I set up the tripod immediately to capture the magnificently illuminated cliffs of Beinn Lair, 2822ft (860m), with Gorm Loch Mor and A'Mhaighdean in the foreground (*pages 48–49*).

At the summer solstice the sun has reached its most north-westerly point at sunset and is perfect for illuminating north-facing corries and cliffs. After this date it begins its journey southward, both at sunrise and sunset. On this midsummer's eve, the air was still at the summit and the silence was total. Reflecting the northern skies over the Outer Hebrides, Fionn Loch turned shades of crimson and yellow as the sun dropped over the edge of the world (*pages 22–23*).

16

AM BUACHAILLE ('THE HERDSMAN'), SANDWOOD BAY, SUTHERLAND

18

SGURR SGIATH AIRIGH, FROM EILEAN A'GHARB-LAIN, LOCH HOURN, KNOYDART

20

LOCH SCAVAIG AND THE BLACK CUILLIN FROM ELGOL, ISLE OF SKYE

22

MIDSUMMER SUNSET ON FIONN LOCH FROM A'MHAIGHDEAN, FISHERFIELD FOREST

24

CAIRN LOCHAN, LOCH MORLICH, CAIRNGORMS NATIONAL NATURE RESERVE

ISLE OF JURA, SOUND OF CORRYVRECKAN FROM SCARBA, ARGYLL

28

OYSTERCATCHER'S NEST, GLEN LYON, BREADALBANE

MELTWATER, GAIRICH, GLEN KINGIE, LOCHABER

30

BEINN DEARG MOR, BEINN DEARG BEAG AND THE SHENAVALL BOTHY, FISHERFIELD FOREST

THE BLACK CUILLIN, ISLE OF SKYE

34

LOCHNAGAR AND THE NORTH-EAST CORRIE, BALMORAL FOREST

36

MARSCO AND BLA BHEINN, GLEN SLIGACHAN, ISLE OF SKYE

TANERA MOR AND TANERA BEG, SUMMER ISLES, FROM MEALL DEARG, SUTHERLAND

40

BEINN BHEOIL, BEN ALDER AND THE LANCET EDGE, LOCH AN SGOIR, BEN ALDER FOREST

+1

42

HOOF OR TINDER FUNGUS ON DEAD BIRCH, GLEN ORCHY

43

TIDAL ROCK POOL, LOCH SUNART, ARDNAMURCHAN

44

LOCH HOURN AND COIRE DHORRCAIL FROM THE SUMMIT OF LADHAR BHEINN, KNOYDART

46

THE SOUND OF LUING: LUNGA, LUING AND SEIL ISLANDS FROM SCARBA, ARGYLL

48

BEINN LAIR AND GORM LOCH MOR FROM THE SUMMIT OF A'MHAIGHDEAN, LETTEREWE FOREST

50

STOER HEAD LIGHTHOUSE, POINT OF STOER, SUTHERLAND

52

SUILVEN, CUL MOR, STAC POLLAIDH, CUL BEAG, BEN MORE COIGACH, ACHNAHAIRD BAY

54

SLIOCH AND ERRATIC BOULDERS, LOCH MAREE, LETTEREWE FOREST

Summer Solstice
to Autumnal Equinox

Irarely set out with the sole intention of photographing a landscape or mountain. My primary purpose is to photograph light, which – like language to a writer – is the means of my creative expression. Once I have selected an area, I plan to visit it at a time of the year when stable weather conditions offer the greatest opportunities to create powerful images. There are, however, no absolute guarantees and frequently, after a cold clear night, my expectations are dashed at dawn, as low cloud begins to form at the summits.

Vertical landscapes, such as Torridon in the far north-west of Scotland, create their own micro-climates. When warm air full of water vapour comes into contact with a colder landmass, clouds form round the mountain peaks, diminishing their potential for photography. Ironically, however, a rapid change in weather conditions can often create a unique combination of light and form that supersedes the original pre-visualized image. Chance is often the extra factor responsible for creating moments in nature that result in outstanding images.

The summer months are always a challenging time for photography. Powerful photographs are the result of contrasts – of light against shadow, of colour against colour and of light against light, and these juxtapositions are fundamental to the success of a composition. But when trees and plants are flourishing in the long hours of daylight, much of the landscape is a profusion of greens. A panoramic image contains a large amount of visual information and if too much is of similar tonal value and texture, the image will fail to inspire. To this end, I need to search for contrasts in the landscape and, in particular, I explore the edges – places where ocean meets land, where mountain peak meets sky or where forest meets river. Environments such as these possess the natural potential from which meaningful images can be created, particularly at the 'magic hours' of dusk and dawn.

The Cuillins on the Isle of Skye offer just such dramatic contrasts and power. They are regarded by many walkers and climbers as the finest single chain of mountains in Britain. Rising straight from the sea to a height of over 3000ft (914m), their eleven Munros offer some of the most challenging climbing in the country. Weather conditions are fickle, with low cloud and sea mists descending without warning. For some time I had visualized a photograph of the main ridge, and spent much time studying maps and relevant climbing books in an effort to identify the optimum viewpoints. One or two possibilities existed but I concluded that Bruach na Frithe, 3143ft (958m), at sunset in late June, would offer excellent potential.

I set off from Sligachan at 3 p.m. and arrived on the summit at around 6.30. The weather was superb and the visibility good, and from the summit the full 7 miles (11km) of ridge lay in front of me. Taking full advantage of the light I set up my camera and photographed the enigmatic spur of rock known as the Basteir Tooth, 3005ft (916m), its black igneous gabbro illuminated by the warm light (*pages 78–79*). As the sun dropped, a reddish light was cast on the ridge and the Cuillin giants – Sgurr a'Ghreadaidh, 3197ft (973m), the Inaccessible Pinnacle, 3235ft (986m), and Sgurr Alasdair, 3255ft (992m) – and I shot a series of images from the summit of Bruach na Frithe (*pages 62–63*). Quickly, I changed to the 180mm lens and in the twilight captured Loch Harpot and MacLeod's Tables (*pages 94–95*). As darkness fell, I returned to the summit and my sleeping bag, which I had arranged in the remains of a rock ice shelter. I lay watching the flickering constellations of the zodiac, savouring each moment before lapsing into sleep.

The seashore provides another marginal environment, rich in visual contrast. For those seeking solitude, the walk to Sandwood Bay in north-west Sutherland is a rewarding one. Lying just to the south of Cape Wrath, the bay is about 4 miles (6.5km) from the road at Oldshore Mor. The white sand beach, bordered by turquoise sea and machair grassland, would not look out of place in a tropical location (*pages 76–77*). If the tide is low, the two flat rock outcrops can be explored. Encrusted with barnacles and limpets, the rocks harbour deep saline channels in which beadlet anemones, sea urchins and kelp survive amidst the perpetual turbulence (*pages 16–17*). The underlying rock is Lewisian gneiss, one of the oldest known, formed 2–3000 million years ago. The other main rock type is Torridonian sandstone: this, being sedimentary, was laid down more recently, around 600 million years ago. To the south-west stands the eroded pinnacle of Am Buachaille ('the Herdsman'), which provides a habitat for nesting fulmars. The Sandwood estate, now owned and protected by the John Muir Trust, is a unique environment with a rich natural diversity.

Driving through Kinlochewe and along the southern shore of Loch Maree, it is impossible not to be moved by the scale of the mountain which dominates the opposite side of the loch (*page 115*). Standing like a fortress at 3218ft (980m), Slioch ('the Hill of Spears') stands between Torridon and the Great Wilderness – the Forests of Letterewe and Fisherfield. Looking south-west, just before Bridge of Grudie, the two giant sentinels Ruadh-stac Mor, 3314ft (1010m) and Sail Mhor, 3218ft (981m), appear to guard the entrance to Coire Mhic Fhearchair, a magnificent natural amphi-theatre scalloped out of the Torridonian sandstone. In the bottom of the corrie lies a loch of the same

name, mirroring the triple buttress that forms the headwall of the corrie. Composed of sandstone and quartzite, it rises to over 985ft (300m) and is one of the finest mountain features in Scotland.

I felt drawn to this area and was intent on producing the definitive image. My first trip in May was essentially exploratory, trying to establish a viewpoint from Beinn a'Chearcaill, 2379ft (725m): it was a washout. I returned in early June, only to be thwarted by a cloudbank to the west, which veiled the sun-light from the mountains at dusk. My third and final trip was just after the summer solstice. Taking into account the north-facing aspect of the mountain, I knew that at midsummer the setting sun would be at its most northerly point of the year and would give the maximum illumination into the corrie.

The weather was settled as I climbed to my viewpoint on Beinn a'Chearcaill. As I waited for the sun to drop, a ptarmigan hen and her five chicks made their way across the plateau, foraging amongst the boulders. By instinct, the mother bird feigned a broken wing in an effort to divert my atten-tion from her brood. Obligingly, I followed her for a short distance before she made an instant 'recovery' and rejoined her young, now at some distance from the potential danger. Like the finding of eagle feathers on Scarba, my encounter with the ptarmigan family brought my experience on this mountain into sharp focus.

Suddenly the sun was dropping and the light reddened. Coire Mhic Fhearchair lit up and the peaks of Rhuadh-stac Mor and Sail Mhor looked majestic in the glow. To the east, Liathach's two Munros – Spidean a'Choire

Leith, 3461ft (1055m), and Mullach an Rathain, 3356ft (1023m), reflected back the dying sunlight (*pages 82–83*).

In the course of numerous trips to the Fisherfield Forest and Torridon, I became aware of a mountain which I believed would offer a superb viewpoint. Beinn Airigh Charr, 2595ft (791m), lies on the north side of Loch Maree in the Letterewe Forest and I was anxious to climb it. On a day during a period of settled weather which I had begun by photographing the dawn at 5.20 a.m. at Sandwood Bay in Sutherland, I decided to attempt the ascent and drove to Poolewe, arriving at 6 p.m.

I set off on foot along the estate road, with time against me, and did not reach the base of the mountain until 8 p.m. I pushed up an excellent stalker's path, but in my haste I ascended a blind summit, lower than the true top, from which I was

unable to see the view south-east to A'Mhaighdean, 3173ft (967m). Frustrated and exhausted, I descended, and reached the road at 10 p.m., still facing a two-hour walk in darkness back to Poolewe. By the time I reached the car I was too cold and tired to pitch a tent and I ended up sleeping in the car near a derelict croft. In the morning I cooked breakfast inside the old ruin and wondered when last someone had prepared a meal in this dwelling – it was an eerie feeling.

A year passed, and this time I was prepared. One day in mid-August we set off in good time from Poolewe and reached the summit at 6 p.m., pitching the tent on a dry mossy flat. The view east across Fionn Loch to An Teallach, 3478ft (1060m), was breathtaking, with Ruadh Stac Mor, 3011ft (918m), A'Mhaighdean and Beinn Tarsuinn, 3070ft (936m) further south. Above Dubh Loch stood Beinn Lair, 2822ft (860m) and Slioch, 3218ft (980m), rising from the shores of Loch Maree across which towered the Torridon giants of Beinn Eighe, 3314ft (1010m), Liathach, 3461ft (1054m), and Beinn Alligin, 3235ft (986m).

As the sun dropped, deep shadows started to form in the glens. A'Mhaighdean's cliffs of Lewisian gneiss reflected back the red light and, above the Causeway and Dubh Loch, the whitewashed walls of the Carnmore Bothy caught the last rays of light (*pages 88–89*).

Below us, foraging in the evening light, was a herd of about forty wild goats. The big males, displaying tall curving horns and long beards, moved progressively closer to us, showing no apparent signs of fear. It wasn't until later that we realized we had pitched our tent in their comfortable, mossy, sleeping area and they weren't for moving. A stand-off ensued with much snorting from one big Billy until a compromise was achieved: we retired to our tent, which allowed the goats to settle for the evening. During the night they grazed and slept all around the tent, as if to prove their point, but by morning they had gone.

59

60

EILEAN MUNDE, LOCH LEVEN AND THE PAP OF GLENCOE, GLEN COE

62

THE BLACK CUILLIN, ISLE OF SKYE

64

— BEINN DEARG, LIATHACH (MULLACH AN RATHAIN AND SPIDEAN A'CHOIRE LEITH) FROM SGURR MHOR, TORRIDON —

66

BEN MORE, ISLE OF MULL AND THE GARVELLACHS, FIRTH OF LORN, ARGYLL

68

BEINN TOAIG AND CLACH LEATHAD, LOCH TULLA, ARGYLL

70

CALEDONIAN PINES, LOCH HOURN, KNOYDART

72

CALEDONIAN PINE TRUNK, GLEN LYON, BREADALBANE

CALEDONIAN PINE CONES, ROTHIEMURCHUS FOREST, CAIRNGORMS

74

BEINN ALLIGIN AND THE HORNS OF ALLIGIN, UPPER LOCH TORRIDON

76

SANDWOOD BAY AND SANDWOOD LOCH, SUTHERLAND

BLACK CUILLIN, AM BASTEIR AND THE BASTEIR TOOTH, ISLE OF SKYE

80

AONACH MOR AND AONACH BEAG FROM SGOR AN LUBHAIR, MAMORES, LOCHABER

82

BEINN EIGHE (RUADH-STAC MOR, SAIL MHOR, LOCH COIRE MHIC FHEARCHAIR)

AND LIATHACH (SPIDEAN A'CHOIRE LEITH AND MULLACH AN RATHAIN), TORRIDON

84

LUNGA, BELNAHUA, FLADDA, LUING AND SEIL ISLANDS, SOUND OF LUING, ARGYLL

LICHENS ON BOULDERS, LOCHAN NA H'ACHALAISE, RANNOCH MOOR

ROCKS AND WATER, RIVER COUPALL, GLEN COE

88

A'MHAIGHDEAN, BEINN LAIR AND FIONN LOCH FROM BEINN AIRIGH CHARR, LETTEREWE FOREST

90

BEINN ALLIGIN, LIATHACH AND BEINN DAMH, LOCH SHIELDAIG

92

BEN NEVIS, CARN MOR DEARG ARÊTE BEYOND THE RING OF STEALL, MAMORES, LOCHABER

94

— LOCH HARPOT AND MACLEOD'S TABLES (HEALABHAL BHEAG AND HEALABHAL MHOR), DUIRINISH, ISLE OF SKYE —

MOONRISE, BLA BHEINN AND SGURR NA STRI, CUILLINS, ISLE OF SKYE

Autumnal Equinox
to Winter Solstice

My passion for wild places did not begin with books or a role model but rather as a fundamental empathy with the natural world. Growing up in a rural area meant I had constant access to the countryside, where I learnt much about nature and the outdoors. As I matured I developed a taste for adventure and soon began to explore the hills and mountains of Central Scotland. In an attempt to capture and share some of my unique mountain experiences, I was drawn to photography. Since then, I have organized my life with photography at its centre, in order to further that passion.

I am often asked what motivates me to climb mountains and photograph them at times when sensible people are comfortably asleep in their beds. Apart from the challenge of being on the summit of a mountain at dusk or dawn, the advantage of height is that the unique features of the surrounding landscape are fully exposed. This should not be confused with aerial photography which, as a result of distance, divorces the viewer from the land.

There is however another reason for my climbs at these hours, which is fundamentally based on physics. Mountains and clouds rising well above the curvature of the earth receive the first rays of light as they skim the horizon some distance away. As they continue back up through the atmospheric filter a second time, their wavelengths of purple and blue are scattered to the extent that they appear

wholly red by the time they reach their subject. The shadows take on a deep bluish purple hue at this time as they are illuminated solely by scattered light. This is the phenomenon known as 'alpenglow' (*opposite*); the reverse happens at sunset (*pages 172-173*). Most of my favourite images have been made at dusk or dawn.

While clouds can threaten photographic opportunities in the mountains, they can also produce exciting images, enhancing the effect of the setting sun. There was a fair amount of cloud around as I left Polldubh at the head of Glen Nevis, where a path climbs through trees above Nevis Gorge to the Steall Meadows (*page 192*). I was climbing with a friend who was keen to experience the challenges of mountain photography. Seven tops over 2950ft (900m) form the great horseshoe known as the Ring of Steall. Not having climbed on this side of the horseshoe before, I was unfamiliar with the landscape and was anxious to find a location for sunset. Passing the spectacular Steall Waterfall, our route took us up the path to An Gearanach, 3221ft (982m), following the high level ridge over An Garbhanach to Stob Coire a'Chairn, 3218ft (981m).

We pushed on to the bealach between Am Bodach, 3386ft (1032m), and Sgor an Lubhair, 3284ft (1001m), where we found an excellent campsite. Although fatigued from carrying heavy rucksacks, we climbed quickly onto the summit of Sgor an Lubhair, carrying only camera equipment. Clouds now obscured the sun, but the sky was a rich collage of pink and purple colours and I set up the camera and tripod in anticipation. Just as it looked as if all would be lost, the sun dropped beneath the clouds and illuminated the summits of Am Bodach and, beyond it, Binnein Beag, 3094ft (943m), in a deep crimson light. I succeeded in shooting two rolls before the sun sank (*pages 102–103*). Elated, we descended to camp, supper and a deep sleep.

For many years I have been obsessed with Torridon and its mountain beauty. The area is the epitome of the Scottish Highlands and I was intent on capturing its essence on film. Having access to the raw material is one thing – albeit four and a half hours from home – but finding the light is another. The weather is notoriously variable due to the proximity of the mountains to the sea and the influence of prevailing westerly winds. Forecasts are seldom sufficiently specific to be reliable.

Shaped and sculpted by ice during the last ice age, these mountains stand in isolation like petrified beasts on the Cambrian plain. Liathach's sheer size and bulk are tremendous; its name means 'the Grey One' and its 5-mile (8km) ridge crosses eight separate tops, two of which are Munros: Spidean a'Choire Leith, 3461ft (1055m), and Mullach an Rathain, 3356ft (1023m). Further to the

99

north-west, Beinn Alligin, 3235ft (986m), with the Horns of Alligin, stands in stark contrast to Liathach, displaying a more feminine character than its neighbour; it is one of my personal favourites. Beinn Eighe, 3314ft (1010m), completes the trio, with seven peaks higher than 3000ft (914m) and the impressive triple buttress Coire Mhic Fhearchair.

Many of the nine trips I made to the area were spent climbing and learning about the landscape. I explored many potential viewpoints, only to discover that when I returned in a different season, the sun was either too low in the sky or set too far north. At one stage I even convinced myself that the definitive image of Liathach had to be shot at dawn from Stuc a'Choire Dhuibh Bhig, 3002ft (915m) at the eastern end of the mountain. This meant climbing by the beam of a head-torch up a challenging route, in snow, for three hours. Having attempted this twice, I gave up on the grounds of safety and resigned myself to finding another option.

Amazingly, I eventually discovered my location for Liathach by chance. Setting off before dawn to shoot Beinn Liath Mhor, 3038ft (926m), and Sgorr Ruadh, 3156ft (962m), we climbed over

moorland and pushed up a steep hill. Nearing the top, I could see rays of pink light illuminating the snow-filled Coire Domhain of Beinn Eighe and as we reached the summit, Liathach appeared in full view and took my breath away. I had found what I had been searching for: the location that put everything in context. Liathach sat majestically, like a king on his throne, rising from Upper Loch Torridon and, to the east, Beinn Eighe appeared in perfect proportion, not overpowering its neighbour in the least. At 14°F (–10°C) the horizontal visibility was crystal clear and I left that summit knowing I had photographed a very special image (*pages 116–117*).

An interest in peaks of lesser stature is a characteristic that sets the mountaineer–photographer apart from those concerned purely with climbing. In order to photograph a Munro or a group of high peaks, I will often ascend a smaller mountain that I consider to offer potential as a viewpoint because it is strategically placed for photography at sunrise or sunset. This is likely to be one of the Corbetts – hills between 2500ft (762m) and 3000ft (914m).

Having climbed much of the Black Cuillin in Skye, I was keen to photograph Sgurr nan Gillean, 3163ft (964m), one of the most prominent peaks on the ridge. From a study of the map, it appeared that Marsco, 2415ft (736m), one of the Red Cuillin, offered the best potential at dawn. We set off, laden with camping equipment, along the Allt Coire nam Bruadaran, picking our way up the south-east ridge of Coire nan Laogh. The weather was clear, with good visibility, but as we neared the summit mist began to form above us, blocking out the summit.

In spite of this disappointment, we decided to push on to the top and within twenty minutes, to our great surprise, we had climbed through the mist. By the time we reached the summit we could see all the neighbouring peaks rising out of the sea of cloud. The views west towards the Black Cuillin were breathtaking, as mist continued to form below us in Glen Sligachan. I set up the camera and shot a series of images of Sgurr nan Gillean as the last rays of sun illuminated the clouds in shades of cerise and yellow (*pages 110–111*). After an overwhelming feeling of despondency, the sensation had now become one of elation and satisfaction. We pitched our tent on a flat grassy area just below the summit. By next morning the cloudbase had dropped and a gale was blowing.

The inclusion of the crofter's house (*page 129*) in this book may seem surprising, since it is essentially a celebration of wild places, devoid of human presence. Although the relevance of this photograph to the portfolio may not be immediately obvious, I felt that it should be included, because the Scottish Highland landscape is not the product of nature alone – indeed many of its wild places are the result of earlier human activities. Large communities of Highlanders once lived in some of the remotest parts of Scotland. In Knoydart, there were sizeable towns in places such as Skiary, Barrisdale, Doune and Airor, where grain and potatoes were grown, but the Clearances changed that.

101

After the Battle of Culloden in 1746, the clan chiefs lost their powers. Many also lost their patriarchal interest in their clansmen and leased their glens and braes to sheep-farmers from the Lowlands and England. As a result, the crofts were cleared of men, women and children, using fire and bayonet to make way for sheep. In Knoydart, approximately 400 people were evicted; their homes were torn down around them and they were herded like animals onto the *Sillary*, a transport ship supplied by the British Government and bound for Canada.

The trend of migration from the land still continues, with farming and fishing in decline. Today the Highlands largely support sporting estates where hunting, shooting and fishing are the main activities. Change is a fundamental principle of life and while I harbour no romantic illusions about the hardship and struggle of surviving in this environment, I often reflect on the direction in which society is heading. Human progress has been made against a backdrop of landscapes transformed to suit the needs of agriculture and industry. Only in recent years have we begun to realize that, rather than defend ourselves against nature, we need to defend nature against ourselves.

102

— RING OF STEALL (AN GEARANACH, AN GARBHANACH, AM BODACH) FROM SGOR AN LUBHAIR, MAMORES, LOCHABER —

CLACH LEATHAD AND MEALL A'BHUIRIDH, LOCHAN NA H'ACHALAISE, RANNOCH MOOR

106

LOCH BEINN A'MHEADHOIN, FASNAKYLE FOREST, GLEN AFFRIC

108

CANISP, SUILVEN, CUL MOR, CUL BEAG AND STAC POLLAIDH, GLENCANISP, SUTHERLAND

SGURR NAN GILLEAN FROM MARSCO, CLOUD INVERSION, CUILLINS, ISLE OF SKYE

112

BUACHAILLE ETIVE MOR AND RIVER ETIVE, GLEN ETIVE

114

HOAR FROST AND SILVER BIRCH, RIVER MERKLAND, SUTHERLAND

15

SLIOCH, LOCH MAREE, LETTEREWE FOREST

116

SGURR DUBH, LIATHACH (SPIDEAN A'CHOIRE LEITH) AND BEINN EIGHE (SGURR BAN,
COIRE DOMHAIN), GLEN TORRIDON

118

BEINN SGRITHEALL, LADHAR BHEINN AND LOCH HOURN, SOUND OF SLEAT, ISLE OF SKYE

120

RIVER ABHAINN DROMA, CORRIESHALLOCH GORGE, BRAEMORE FOREST

122

STOB COIRE AN LAOIGH, AONACH BEAG, AONACH MOR AND BEN NEVIS FROM
STOB CHOIRE CLAURIGH, GREY CORRIES, LOCHABER

123

124

THE CUILLIN RIDGE FROM GLEN DRYNOCH, ISLE OF SKYE

126

GARBH BHEINN, LOCH LINNIE, ARDGOUR

128

BEINN ALLIGIN (TOM NA GRUAGAICH AND SGURR MHOR), UPPER LOCH TORRIDON

DERELICT CROFT, GARVE, WESTER ROSS

130

LOCH AN EILEIN AND ROTHIEMURCHUS FOREST, GLEN FESHIE

132

PAP OF GLENCOE, SGORR NAM FIANNAIDH, BALLACHULISH, LOCH LEVEN

134

BEINN FHADA, SAILEAG, SGURR A'BHEALAICH DHEIRG, AONACH MHEADHOIN,
CISTE DHUBH, GLEN SHIEL, KINTAIL

136

CUL MOR, STAC POLLAIDH, CUL BEAG AND BEN MORE COIGACH, ACHNAHAIRD BAY

STOB GHABHAR, LOCH TULLA, INVERORAN, ARGYLL

Winter Solstice
to Vernal Equinox

The approach of the winter solstice is the signal for me to pay close attention to the weather affecting specific mountains. I had attempted to photograph Beinn Alligin in Torridon on several occasions, but had always been prevented by deteriorating weather conditions. It is a beautifully sculpted mountain and can be seen to advantage across Upper Loch Torridon, from just above the Torridon Hotel. Known as 'the Jewelled Mountain', its two most distinctive features are the spectacular Eag Dhubh – 'the Black Cleft' – and Nan Rathanan, 'the Horns of Alligin' (*pages 74–75 and 128*). Having already made an ascent in August (*pages 64–65*), I visualized an image at sunset from Tom na Gruagaich, 3025ft (922m), over the Torridon Forest, with warm autumnal colours and a dusting of snow on the summits. Two years passed before I managed to be in the right place at the right time.

Setting off at 11 a.m. we arrived on the summit of Tom na Gruagaich at 1.15 p.m. to an awesome view. The conditions were near perfect. Looking north-east across Nan Rathanan stood Ben Dearg, 3000ft (914m), and beyond, in the Fisherfield Forest, the snow-covered cliffs of A'Mhaighdean, 3173ft (967m), were visible. To the east, Slioch's 3218ft (981m) fortressed summit caught the setting sun. Further east, the summit ridge of the Torridon giant Beinn Eighe, 3314ft

(1010m), snaked into the distance and, just out of shot, the ridge of Liathach, 3356ft (1023m), fell into shadow. I set up the tripod and shot continually as the sun dropped in the sky, the clouds creating a constantly changing pattern of light and shadow on the landscape (*pages 148–149*).

To witness a peregrine stoop is one of the high points of mountain experience. I recall near Loch na Sealga in the Fisherfield Forest watching a soaring bird high above its hunting territory, looking too remote to be menacing. Suddenly, wings drawn in, it dropped like a stone towards its unsuspecting quarry. High in Glen Lee, I have also watched peregrine and eagle working as a team. While the eagle quartered the moorland in the lower air – its size effective at flushing grouse from the heather – far above it soared the peregrine, a moustached killer that plummeted earthward at the first sight of quarry. The symbiosis continued until both were satisfied.

In the clear, crisp atmosphere of a winter dawn, the contrasts in the mountain landscape are at their sharpest and most dramatic. I was keen to photograph the Five Sisters of Kintail from an easterly aspect, at dawn, originally identifying Saileag, 3136ft (956m), as the most probable point. There has always been, for me, an enigma surrounding Kintail. I find it silent and timeless, like a forgotten place, and I was anxious to preserve this quality in the images I planned. Walking in the mountains during the summer months is the most effective way of understanding the landscape, particularly if you plan to return in the winter for additional drama. Often however, it is difficult to visualize the exact position of the sun at sunrise or sunset and the extent of its illumination, given its considerably lower altitude. Experience comes into play in the process of visualizing an approximation of the scene. Panoramic images require that the balance of light and shadow affecting the composition should favour light. If the overwhelming impression from an image is one of darkness, it will not be successful.

In spite of my plan, when the time came in early January, I found myself above the Bealach na Lapain at 7.50 a.m. in freezing conditions, doubting my original judgment. Impulsively, I aborted the ascent of Saileag and headed for the ridge and Sgurr nan Spainteach, 3247ft (990m). The great north-east corrie, drained by the Allt a'Choire Dhomdain, was in deep shadow and it was likely to remain that way for most of the day, due to the low altitude of the sun.

Reaching the summit of Sgurr nan Spainteach, the view north-west was spectacular, with low cloud brushing the sum-

mits. To the east on the other side of the glen. Sgurr na Sgine, 3100ft (945m), and the Saddle. 3314ft (1010m), were already in the sunlight. Immediately in front of me stood Sgurr na Ciste Duibhe, 3369ft (1027m), and, to the north, Sgurr Fhuaran, 3501ft (1067m), its summit trailing a white plume. As the sun rose the light changed from pink to yellow and then cleared, and I waited until the sun had risen sufficiently to achieve the necessary balance of light and shadow (*pages 150–151*). Had I pursued my original goal of shooting from Saileag, the deep areas of shadow in the corrie would have overpowered the image.

I faced a similar problem when photographing Ben Nevis. I had spent some time in and around the surrounding mountains and had identified the summit of Carn Mor Dearg, 4003ft (1220m), as offering the best potential viewpoint. At 4409ft (1344m), Ben Nevis is the highest mountain in the British Isles and is a remarkably difficult one to photograph. Its spectacular north-east face is hidden from all but a few viewpoints; indeed, the tourist route up the mountain is a sure way not to see it. Rising vertically from the Allt a'Mhuilinn, Coire na Ciste embodies some of the best-known climbing routes in the country: Zero Gully, Observatory Ridge and Tower Gully are a few examples.

My father and I set off in early September to research a location and camped overnight on the summit of Carn Mor Dearg, identifying two points to which we would return in winter. My main problem was a familiar one: I needed good snow and ice to create the drama I visualized, combined with a spring sunrise – in fact, a sunrise as late in the season as I could hope for. As the spring equinox approaches the sun is progressively rising further north each morning, allowing more light to reach the north-east face at dawn. The downside is that sunrise gets earlier every morning.

I waited until a sustained cold period at the end of February created perfect conditions in the area. Good weather was forecast for the next three days and we drove immediately to Fort William and checked in at the Distillery House. We planned to leave at 4 a.m. the following day, 1 March, and climb to the summit of Carn Mor Dearg, where I hoped to photograph the dawn at around 7.30. It was a sleepless, if short, night. Outside the temperature was 14°F (–10°C) and the weather and conditions were perfect. The only thing not perfect was me, as I was suffering a nasty bout of flu. Despite my high temperature, we set off into the darkness: our world reduced to the circular beams of light from our head-torches. I struggled, and seriously considered turning back on several occasions, but the thought that I might have to re-live this experience at some time in the future kept me going.

Soon we were walking in crampons, making better progress on the ice as the daylight approached. Fatigued, we arrived on the summit of Carn Dearg

Meadhonach, 3871ft (1180m), where I set up the first shot. The conditions were superb: the sun was already up, but needed to rise further in order to illuminate the lower reaches of Ben Nevis's north-east face. By 9 a.m. it was as good as it was going to get, and I shot through five rolls before traversing to Carn Mor Dearg. From there I took another series of photographs which included the Carn Mor Dearg arête and Coire Leis. The shoot was an unprecedented success, although I couldn't help wishing that more light had illuminated the face at sunrise – but that was a factor beyond my control (*pages 144–145*).

Finally, there are few mountains in Scotland that invoke such a feeling of utter wildness as An Teallach 3478ft (1060m). Seen in winter across Loch Droma, the mountain rises vertically in terraces of red sandstone to a sharply pinnacled summit ridge. Early views inspired in me a desire to explore this enigmatic mountain, which appears far more complex when viewed from its base. My first ascent was made during a period of fine weather in early May. Starting from the Dundonnell Hotel, we climbed in a counter-clockwise circuit: a route that I maintain offers the best aspects of the mountain. Astonishingly, just below the summit of Corrag Bhuide, 3435ft (1047m), we came across the most perfectly preserved plant fossil in a large boulder – it seems incredible that something that originated at the bottom of an ocean should be discovered at such a height.

Rather than satisfying my ambitions regarding this mountain, that first sortie fuelled a further desire to photograph the southern tops in winter, from the summit of Bidein a'Ghlas Thuill, 3484ft (1062m), at sunrise. Estimating that the optimum time for photography would be around mid-February, I calculated that it would require a departure at around 4.45 a.m. to reach the summit by dawn. Three years would pass before I succeeded. Before my second attempt, I recall driving up to Dundonnell on a very clear evening and seeing the well-defined summit ridge in the moonlight. My confidence was high but the following morning there was a rather disturbing wind at sea level. By the time I had climbed about halfway, the wind was reaching gale force. Clouds began to fill the sky and I gave up the attempt.

The following year however, I succeeded, climbing in the circular beam of a head-torch for the first 90 minutes and using crampons from sea level. The last push up to the summit of Bidein a'Ghlas Thuill was exhausting, but the view, hidden until I reached the top, was awesome (pages 158–159). Pink light illuminated Sgurr Fiona, 3478ft (1060m), Lord Berkley's Seat, 3379ft (1030m), and Loch Toll an Lochain. Ice crystals glistened in the air. Further off, the peaks of Fisherfield Forest stood in their arctic mantle: Beinn Dearg Mor, 2986ft (910m), Ruadh Stac Mor, 3012ft (918m) and A'Mhaighdean, 3173ft (967m). I descended, content that I had experienced the sublime high point of Scotland's wild places

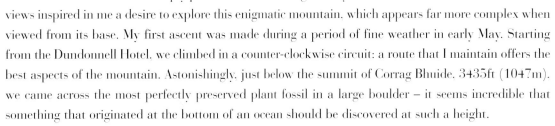

THE THREE SISTERS, PASS OF GLENCOE

144

BEN NEVIS, COIRE NA CISTE FROM CARN MOR DEARG, LOCHABER

146

MOONRISE, LOCHAN NA H'ACHALAISE AND LOCH BA, RANNOCH MOOR

148

SGURR NA SGINE, THE SADDLE AND FIVE SISTERS OF KINTAIL (SGURR NA
CISTE DUIBHE, SGURR FHUARAN), GLEN SHIEL, KINTAIL

152

SUILVEN, CANISP, CUL MOR, LOCH SIONASCAIG FROM STAC POLLAIDH, INVERPOLLY NATURE RESERVE

154

BEINN AN DOTHAIDH, BEN DORAIN, BEN MORE, STOB BINNEIN, CRUACH ARDRAIN, BEINN A'CHROIN,
AN CAISTEAL, BEINN CHABHAIR FROM STOB GHABHAR, ARGYLL

156

THE COBBLER (BEN ARTHUR). ARROCHAR. ARGYLL

157

BEN LOMOND AND LOCH LOMOND, LUSS, ARGYLL

158

AN TEALLACH (SGURR FIONA, LORD BERKLEY'S SEAT AND CORRAG BHUIDE)
FROM BIDEIN A'GHLAS THUILL, FISHERFIELD FOREST

160

ST CYRUS NATURE RESERVE, ABERDEENSHIRE

BIDEAN NAM BIAN, BUACHAILLE ETIVE MOR, GLEN ETIVE FROM STOB GHABHAR, ARGYLL

164

BEN LOMOND AND LOCH LOMOND FROM BEINN DUBH, LUSS, ARGYLL

166

LIATHACH (SPIDEAN A'CHOIRE LEITH) AND BEINN EIGHE, LOCH CLAIR, GLEN TORRIDON

BUACHAILLE ETIVE MOR (STOB DEARG), RIVER ETIVE, GLEN ETIVE

170

ROCKS AND ICE, RIVER ETIVE, GLEN ETIVE

BUACHAILLE ETIVE MOR, RIVER ETIVE, GLEN ETIVE

172

BAOSBHEINN AND SGURR MHOR, SHIELDAIG FOREST, TORRIDON

174

ARKLE, LOCH STACK, REAY FOREST, SUTHERLAND

176

STOB COIRE EASAIN, STOB A'CHOIRE MHEADHION, BEYOND GEAL CHARN, BEINN A'CHLACHAIR, BEINN EIBHINN, AONACH BEAG, GEAL-CHARN, BEN ALDER, SCHIEHALLION, FROM STOB CHOIRE CLAURIGH, GREY CORRIES, LOCHABER

178

SGURR A'BHEALAICH DHEIRG, AONACH MHEADHOIN, CISTE DHUBH, LOCH CLUANIE, GLEN SHIEL

THE MOUNTAINS OF LOCHABER FROM STOB CHOIRE CLAURIGH, GREY CORRIES, LOCHABER

*Numbers on the map refer to the page
numbers of the relevant photographs*

John o'Groats

Thurso

Wick

Tongue

Kinlochbervie

76
16
58

174

Stornoway

50

108

114

52
136
38

152

Tarbert

Ullapool

Fraserburgh

158
30

Poolewe

88
48
22

Banff

Gairloch

101
54

64
59
115
82

129

Dingwall

120

Elgin

172
148
166
116

Achnasheen

Peterhead

90
128
74

Nairn

INVERNESS

Portree

14

124
36
110
94
78

Kyle of Lochalsh

106

32
62
96

118

140
150

178

Fort Augustus

Aviemore

24
130
73

ABERDEEN

18
70

134

44

13

Ballater

20

29

142

Mallaig

34

Stonehaven

180
176

40

FORT WILLIAM

144
92

122

80
102

160

PHOTOGRAPHIC NOTE

'An image doesn't start with a camera – it ends there.' is a useful maxim borrowed from one of the National Geographic Photographer's Field Guides. Its simple, concise message serves to remind photographers that it is what lies 'beyond the lens' that should command their attention. Nevertheless, for each assignment, it is essential to have the right photographic equipment at hand, together with an understanding of its limitations.

Cameras, just like any other tools, are designed to operate within a range of parameters to fulfil different criteria. The choice of equipment depends largely on subject-matter, personal preference and the ability of the camera to reproduce the image visualized by the photographer. I have experimented with camera formats for many years, and maintain that they are an important and often overlooked aspect of the visualization process. Like an artist's canvas, the shape and size of the film, onto which the photographer paints with light, is an important aspect of the total image.

The panoramic format delivers a powerful visual experience. Its 3:1 image ratio is superb for composing landscape using the rule of thirds. I find that it depicts the way I see the world and gives poignancy to my work. I have also owned and used most other camera formats and have a distinct preference for rectangular formats. Recently, I worked with a Fuji GX680 system (6 x 8 format) but found it too bulky for location work. I followed it with a Linhof Technikardan 5 x 4, but was frustrated by the length of time that it took to set up the camera, often missing the conditions which had inspired the photography in the first place. I now use an Arca Swiss 6 x 9, which I find superb. Like the Linhof 5 x 4 it has a telescopic monorail and full camera movements, but it uses 6 x 9 roll-film backs, which are infinitely quicker than the sheet film used by the Linhof 5 x 4. While the camera is still reasonably bulky and heavy, it is by comparison faster to set up and produces transparencies of outstanding brilliance, through a range of Schneider lenses.

My early work was with 35mm Nikon cameras and I found their 24 x 36mm format well suited to all aspects of photography. Certainly the 3:2 ratio produced pleasing results, both for landscape and for the underwater images I was shooting at the time. Working underwater is a very different challenge from landscape photography, but I learnt some interesting lessons from this pursuit which I still use today. In order to cope with the additional problems posed by taking photographs underwater, I organized my diving and photographic equipment in such a way that it became 'invisible' – not physically, but philosophically. In an effort to maximize every possible photo opportunity underwater, I built camera systems which performed with 100 per cent reliability and sourced diving equipment in which I put the same confidence. For a photographer, there is little point in being deep under the Red Sea as a shoal of hammerhead sharks passes, if you then find that you are having trouble with your regulator or that your flash won't fire.

In the mountains I use the same philosophy, paying the same attention to detail in both photo-graphic and mountaineering equipment. In winter conditions, crampons, an ice axe and a head-torch are as essential as the camera and tripod. All the images published in this book have been shot with the aid of a tripod. Image sharpness has as much to do with camera shake as it has with lens design, and a tripod is essential if depth of field is to be maximized. During the last three years I have carried the superb Gitzo Mountaineer carbon fibre tripod with a 3-D head. This is consider-ably lighter than its alloy equivalent, which has been a welcome development as weight remains the limiting factor on many of my excursions, particularly if camping equipment is added. The film stock I use is exclusively Fuji Velvia, which produces a highly saturated transparency, rich in greens and blacks. Normally rated at 40ASA, the exposure latitude is narrow and the emulsion is intoler-ant of erroneous exposure readings.

Most of my work is now shot on a Fuji GX617, using either the standard 90mm f5.6 or the 180mm f6.7 lens. Originally designed by Linhof, a panoramic model by Fuji was introduced some years later with some notable improvements – namely, an ergonomic design, interchangeable lens-es protected by an aluminium frame, detachable high-magnification viewfinder, film-winding crank and a vertically opening back. The lenses produce transparencies of outstanding brilliance and colour balance, free of chromatic aberrations. On most trips, I carry both lenses and around thirty rolls of 120 film.

HUGH PRIOR

Much of my time in the mountains has been spent with my father. We have shared many of the high points of mountain experience in remote locations at dusk and dawn. Whether under canvas, in a bothy, or in some grim motel on the edge of nowhere, our shared expeditions have helped us to develop a special relationship. The photography of wild places requires commitment and a certain amount of tenacity – to photograph a mountain such as Ben Nevis from the 4003ft (1220m) Carn Mor Dearg in March at dawn demands a 4 a.m. departure and a three-and-a-half-hour uphill walk in the circular beam of a head-torch to reach the summit. What might to other companions have seemed ludicrous was always accepted without protest by my father, whose spiritual and physical support has been a constant source of encouragement to me. I am indebted to him for his unfailing energy, which has helped me to capture the dramatic mountain landscapes of Scotland, Pakistan, Nepal, India and Patagonia.

NOTES ON THE PHOTOGRAPHS

All photographs taken with the panoramic Fuji GX617 fitted with the SWD90mm f5.6 wideangle make use of the dedicated centre filter for this lens. The filter distributes light evenly from corner to corner and prevents vignetting. To compensate for light loss the aperture must opened by one stop. When determining exposure, aperture always takes priority, as the performance of large format lenses is enhanced by the use of small apertures. Similarly, foreground sharpness is improved with the increased depth of field that results from using a small aperture. As the camera is always mounted on a Gitzo Mountaineer tripod, the difference between ¼ and ½ second is of no significance. I deviate from this principle only if I have to consider camera shake in a high wind, particularly when using the W180mm f6.7 lens, or if I have to take account of the movement of waves: shutter speed then becomes a greater consideration. Exposures are made with a Minolta Auto Meter IVF, generally in the range of 1 second to ¼ second at between f16–f32. Film stock is Fuji Velvia, rated at 40ASA.

VERNAL EQUINOX TO SUMMER SOLSTICE
(20–21 March to 20–22 June)

midsummer sun reaches the furthest point north-west at which it will set, before resuming its journey south in the endless cycle of seasons.

Gairich, meltwater flows to the River Kingie to reach Loch Quoich. Remote and desolate, Glen Kingie runs eastwards into Glen Garry.

pages 16–17   Am Buachaille ('The Herdsman'), Sandwood Bay, Sutherland
Date 19 May 1999 *Time* 6.10 a.m. *Camera* Fuji GX617 *Lens* SWD90mm f5.6
Having camped overnight at Sandwood Loch, I rose at dawn to set up the camera on a rock outcrop on the beach. Against a flooding tide I shot towards Am Buachaille, which is home to colonies of breeding fulmars and gannets.

pages 18–19   Sgurr Sgiath Airigh, 2890ft (881m), from Eilean a'Gharb-lain, Loch Hourn, Knoydart
Date 9 May 1995 *Time* 10.40 a.m. *Camera* Fuji GX617 *Lens* SWD90mm f5.6
An early morning boat trip took us onto the largest of the four islands in Loch Hourn, which supports a big seal colony and resident barn owls. As two golden eagles displayed high above, a cuckoo called from the neighbouring shores.

pages 20–21   Loch Scavaig and the Black Cuillin from Elgol, Isle of Skye
Date 5 June 1995 *Time* 1.10 p.m. *Camera* Fuji GX617 *Lens* SWD90mm f5.6
This viewpoint has to be one of the best in Europe. The photograph was taken in the middle of the day, to take advantage of the high sun reflecting on the barnacles below the water. The turquoise sea creates an excellent setting for the ultimate mountains.

pages 22–23   Midsummer sunset over Fionn Loch from A'Mhaighdean, 3173ft (967m), Fisherfield Forest
Date 21 June 1995 *Time* 10.40 p.m. *Camera* Fuji GX617 *Lens* W180mm f6.7
A spectacular evening to celebrate the summer solstice from Britain's remotest mountain. The

pages 24–25   Cairn Lochan, 3986ft (1215m), Loch Morlich, Cairngorms National Nature Reserve
Date 4 April 1995 *Time* 7.20 a.m. *Camera* Fuji GX617 *Lens* SWD90mm f5.6
Loch Morlich is a classic example of a 'kettle hole' – a water-filled depression which marks the final resting-place of a massive fragment of ice. It became embedded in gravel and sand, forming a cavity which filled with water as the ice thawed.

pages 26–27   Isle of Jura, Sound of Corryvreckan from Scarba, Argyll
Date 18 June 2000 *Time* 6.50 a.m. *Camera* Fuji GX617 *Lens* W180mm f6.7
Having camped overnight on Scarba to photograph the Sound of Luing, I turned my attention south-west to Jura at dawn. The early morning air was clear and moist and I shot this desolate coastline with the 'Paps' beyond.

page 28   Oystercatcher's nest, Glen Lyon, Breadalbane
Date 19 April 1996 *Time* 2.20 p.m. *Camera* Hasselblad 503CX *Lens* Zeiss Makro-Planar CF 120mm f4
Having watched the female bird through binoculars for some time, I quickly set up this photograph being careful not to disturb her. The nest was on a shingle riverbank and the eggs were almost invisible in their environment. I like the simplicity of this image.

page 29   Meltwater, Gairich, 3015ft (919m), Glen Kingie, Lochaber
Date 27 April 1996 *Time* 10.40 a.m. *Camera* Hasselblad 503CX *Lens* Zeiss Planar CF 150mm f4
From snowfields on the mountain ridges of

pages 30–31   Beinn Dearg Mor, 2986ft (910m), Beinn Dearg Beag, 2690ft (820m), and the Shenavall Bothy, Fisherfield Forest
Date 20 June 1995 *Time* 6.20 a.m. *Camera* Fuji GX617 *Lens* SWD90mm f5.6
After a night in the midge-infested bothy, I rose to a bright clear dawn. Waiting for the sun to clear the ridges of An Teallach, 3478ft (1060m), behind, I watched a peregrine falcon mounting the air above Loch na Sealga before plummeting earthwards.

pages 32–33   The Black Cuillin: Sgurr a'Mhadaidh, 3012ft (918m), Sgurr a'Ghreadaidh, 3197ft (973m), Sgurr na Banachdich, 3166ft (965m), Sgurr Dearg, 3235ft (986m), Sgurr Mhic Choinnich, 3110ft (948m), Sgurr Alasdair, 3255ft (992m), Sgurr Dubh Mor, 3097ft (944m), Gars-bheinn, 2936ft (895m), Isle of Skye
Date 18 June 1995 *Time* 4.40 a.m. *Camera* Fuji GX617 *Lens* SWD90mm f5.6
I photographed the Cuillin Ridge at dawn after a bivouac on the summit of Sgurr a'Mhadaidh. As the sun rose, an inversion lay below me above the waters of Loch Coruisk. The summit of Sgurr Alasdair is clearly visible, with the Cuillin of Rhum beyond.

pages 34–35   Lochnagar, 3789ft (1155m), and the north-east corrie, Balmoral Forest
Date 6 April 2000 *Time* 7.10 a.m. *Camera* Fuji GX617 *Lens* W180mm f6.7
Photographed at sunrise, the great north-east corrie is illuminated with red light. Although this is a regular occurrence on the geological time scale, recording it took three years for a mere mortal to achieve.

pages 36–37 **Marsco, 2415ft (736m), and Bla Bheinn (Blaven), 3045ft (928m), Glen Sligachan, Isle of Skye**

Date 5 June 1995 *Time* 9.20 p.m. *Camera* Fuji GX617 *Lens* SWD90mm f5.6

This image, shot late on a summer's evening, captures the last rays of light on Marsco and Blaven and highlights the benefit of being at high altitude at dusk and dawn. Within minutes my foreground light had gone, yet on the tops it would linger for some time.

pages 38–39 **Tanera Mor and Tanera Beg, Summer Isles, from Meall Dearg, 535ft (163m), Sutherland**

Date 19 May 1999 *Time* 9.10 p.m. *Camera* Fuji GX617 *Lens* W180mm f6.7

The islands known collectively as the Summer Isles are composed of Torridonian sandstone. Photographed at dusk from Meall Dearg near Dornie, the spectacular peaks of the Letterewe and Fisherfield Forests can be seen beyond.

pages 40–41 **Beinn Bheoil, 3343ft (1019m), Ben Alder, 3766ft (1148m), and the Lancet Edge, Loch an Sgoir, Ben Alder Forest**

Date 8 June 1995 *Time* 6.10 a.m. *Camera* Fuji GX617 *Lens* SWD90mm f5.6

Following a third night on the summit of Carn Dearg, 3392ft (1034m), the weather cleared and I was confronted with a clear dawn. The view south-west shows the Lancet Edge and, beyond, the pass known as Bealach Dubh.

page 42 **Hoof or tinder fungus (Fomes fomentarius) on dead birch, Glen Orchy**

Date 16 April 1996 *Time* 11.40 a.m. *Camera* Hasselblad 503CX *Lens* Zeiss Planar CFE 80mm f2.8

This image highlights the symbiosis that exists in nature: one species depends on the death of another for its survival. The spores from these fungi will in turn colonize another dead birch.

page 43 **Tidal rock pool, Loch Sunart, Ardnamurchan**

Date 12 May 1996 *Time* 10.10 a.m. *Camera* Hasselblad 503CX *Lens* Zeiss Makro-Planar CF 120mm f4

Rockpools support a population of seemingly alien life-forms, with strange textures, smells and colours, which inhabit the inter-tidal zone. They have always fascinated me, and images like this one have the power to trigger memories from my childhood.

pages 44–45 **Loch Hourn and Coire Dhorrcail from the summit of Ladhar Bheinn, 3346ft (1020m), Knoydart**

Date 10 May 1995 *Time* 9.10 a.m. *Camera* Fuji GX617 *Lens* SWD90mm f5.6

Early mists can be a bitter disappointment

when photography is planned for sunrise, as they often take hours to burn off. After an early start, I waited nearly 1½ hours before there was sufficient clarity to shoot, but the result is not without drama.

pages 46–47 **The Sound of Luing: Lunga, Luing and Seil islands from Scarba, Argyll**

Date 17 June 2000 *Time* 8.20 p.m. *Camera* Fuji GX617 *Lens* W180mm f6.7

The view north-west at sunset from the summit of Scarba includes the islands of Lunga, Belnahua, Fladda, Seil and Luing. To the north lies Loch Linnie, with Ben Nevis, 4409ft (1344m), and the Grey Corries. Note the strength of the ebb tide in the Sound of Luing.

pages 48–49 **Beinn Lair, 2822ft (860m), and Gorm Loch Mor from the summit of A'Mhaighdean, 3173ft (967m), Letterewe Forest**

Date 21 June 1995 *Time* 7.45 p.m. *Camera* Fuji GX617 *Lens* SWD90mm f5.6

Beinn Lair possesses the longest wall of unbroken cliffs in the Highlands. This peak, Ruadh Stac Mor, 3011ft (918m), and A'Mhaighdean are the remotest mountains in Britain.

pages 50–51 **Stoer Head Lighthouse, Point of Stoer, Sutherland**

Date 9 April 1999 *Time* 11.10 a.m. *Camera* Fuji GX617 *Lens* W180mm f6.7

Prevailing north-westerlies batter the coastline continuously. Stoer Head Lighthouse stands on a desolate headland overlooking the Minch. A Force 7 gale was blowing as I arrived and I struggled to prevent my tripod blowing over.

pages 52–53 **Suilven, 2398ft (731m), Cul Mor, 2785ft (849m), Stac Pollaidh, 2011ft (613m), Cul Beag, 2523ft (769m), Ben More Coigach, 2438ft (743m), Achnahaird Bay**

Date 19 May 1999 *Time* 7.20 p.m. *Camera* Fuji GX617 *Lens* SWD90mm f5.6

The sea cliffs to the west of this bay support a large colony of shags, and peregrines can be seen heeling over the stacks and sending seabirds into panic. The juxtaposition of Inverpolly Nature Reserve with the marine environment is a powerful one.

pages 54–55 **Slioch, 3218ft (980m), and erratic boulders, Loch Maree, Letterewe Forest**

Date 15 May 1995 *Time* 7.50 p.m. *Camera* Fuji GX617 *Lens* SWD90mm f5.6

This area of erratics – boulders deposited in glacial moraines – offers endless possibilities for compositions. The red Torridonian sandstone has been sculpted into textured rocks of all shapes and sizes, a perfect foreground for Slioch's fortress summit.

SUMMER SOLSTICE TO AUTUMNAL EQUINOX
(20–22 June to 22–24 September)

pages 60–61 **Eilean Munde, Loch Leven and the Pap of Glencoe, 2434ft (742m), Glen Coe**

Date 21 August 1994 *Time* 7.30 a.m. *Camera* Fuji GX617 *Lens* SWD90mm f5.6

An early rise at 5.30 produced no results – the cloudbase was low and thick mist covered the peaks. By 7.30, however, the mist was burning off, creating a superb scene. Eilean Munde is the ancient burial ground of Clan MacDonald.

pages 62–63 **The Black Cuillin: Bidean Druim nan Ramh, 2851ft (869m), Sgurr a'Mhadaidh, 3012ft (918m), Sgurr a'Ghreadaidh, 3197ft (973m), Sgurr na Banachdich, 3166ft (965m), Sgurr Dearg, 3235ft (986m), Sgurr Mhic Choinnich, 3110ft (948m), Sgurr Alasdair, 3255ft (992m), Sgurr Dubh Mor, 3097ft (944m), Gars-bheinn, 2936ft (895m), Isle of Skye**

Date 28 June 1995 *Time* 9.50 p.m. *Camera* Fuji GX617 *Lens* SWD90mm f5.6

Late in the evening from the summit of Bruach na Frithe, 3143ft (958m), I shot a series of images of the main ridge, including the Cuillin Giants – Sgurr a'Ghreadaidh, Sgurr Dearg (the Inaccessible Pinnacle) and Sgurr Alasdair – illuminated by a reddish light.

pages 64–65 **Beinn Dearg, 3000ft (914m), Liathach: Mullach an Rathain, 3356ft (1023m), and Spidean a'Choire Leith, 3461ft (1055m), from Sgurr Mhor, 3235ft (985m), Torridon**

Date 8 August 1999 *Time* 4.20 p.m. *Camera* Fuji GX617 *Lens* SWD90mm f5.6

Having climbed to Tom na Gruagaich, 3025ft (922m), and passed Eag Dhubh, we arrived on the summit of Sgurr Mhor. The scale of the landscape is tremendous, with views to Ben Dearg, Mullach an Rathain and Spidean a'Choire Leith on Liathach.

pages 66–67 **Ben More, 3169ft (966m), Isle of Mull and the Garvellachs, Firth of Lorn, Argyll**

Date 17 July 2000 *Time* 9.50 p.m. *Camera* Fuji GX617 *Lens* W180mm f6.7

The Isles of the Sea – also known as the Garvellachs – contain ecclesiastical antiquities, including the remains of a monastery, predating those on Iona of AD 542. Silhouetted beyond is Ben More on the Isle of Mull.

pages 68–69 **Beinn Toaig, 2736ft (834m), and Clach Leathad, 3602ft (1098m), Loch Tulla, Argyll**

Date 22 August 2000 *Time* 1.20 p.m. *Camera* Fuji GX617 *Lens* SWD90mm f5.6

I was drawn to the tranquillity of this scene,

which epitomizes a Scottish summer's day. Fleets of cumulus clouds drifting over the landscape were reflected in the tranquil waters of Loch Tulla. I shot a series of images before the Scottish midge drew first blood.

pages 70–71 Caledonian pines, Loch Hourn, Knoydart

Date 3 September 2000 *Time* 5.40 p.m. *Camera* Fuji GX617 *Lens* SWD90mm f5.6

The groups of Caledonian pines on the shores of Loch Hourn are of a species unique to Scotland. Having grown up in isolation, these venerable trees share a genus with similar species growing in Scandinavia, where they are thought to have originated, and from where they were carried by the ice sheet during the last ice age.

page 72 Caledonian pine trunk, Glen Lyon, Breadalbane

Date 17 September 1997 *Time* 11.10 a.m. *Camera* Hasselblad 503CX *Lens* Zeiss Makro-Planar CF 120mm f4

This image is an exploration of the complex relationships that exist in the natural world, which can take many forms: some are opportunistic and some symbiotic, while others are parasitic.

page 73 Caledonian pine cones, Rothiemurchus Forest, Cairngorms

Date 17 September 1998 *Time* 2.20 p.m. *Camera* Hasselblad 503CX *Lens* Zeiss Makro-Planar CF 120mm f4

This study of pattern and texture provided by a crop of Scots pine cones gathered on the ground symbolizes rejuvenation and growth. The cones form part of the staple diet of the native crossbill, which uses its specially adapted bill to remove the seeds

pages 74–75 Beinn Alligin, 3235ft (986m), and the Horns of Alligin, Upper Loch Torridon

Date 23 July 2000 *Time* 3.00 p.m. *Camera* Fuji GX617 *Lens* SWD90mm f5.6

Beinn Alligin, the 'Jewelled Hill', is a beautifully sculpted mountain, seen to best advantage across Upper Loch Torridon. It has a more feminine character than its muscle-bound neighbours Liathach, 3461ft (1054m), and Beinn Eighe, 3314ft (1010m).

pages 76–77 Sandwood Bay and Sandwood Loch, Sutherland

Date 7 August 1999 *Time* 8.40 a.m. *Camera* Fuji GX617 *Lens* SWD90mm f5.6

Isolated by distance, Sandwood Bay is a wild environment rich in geology and wildlife – the underlying rocks are of Lewisian gneiss, laid down 3000 million years ago. I timed my visit knowing that the tide would be at full ebb at dawn, exposing the sands.

pages 78–79 Black Cuillin, Am Basteir, 3143ft (958m) and the Basteir Tooth, Isle of Skye

Date 28 June 1995 *Time* 8.10 p.m. *Camera* Fuji GX617 *Lens* SWD90mm f5.6

I was keen to photograph the enigmatic spur of rock known as the Basteir Tooth. As the sun set, my own shadow was projected on the rocks and in a strange way I suddenly felt part of the celestial movements.

pages 80–81 Aonach Mor, 4006ft (1221m), and Aonach Beag, 4049ft (1234m), from Sgor an Lubhair, 3284ft (1001m), Mamores, Lochaber

Date 28 August 2000 *Time* 7.40 a.m. *Camera* Fuji GX617 *Lens* W180mm f6.7

Following a high camp on Am Bodach, I awoke to a rather overcast morning. As the sun rose, the cloud dispersed quickly and I was able to photograph both the Aonachs, Carn Mor Dearg, 4003ft (1223m), and Ben Nevis, 4409ft (1344m).

pages 82–83 Beinn Eighe: Ruadh-stac Mor, 3314ft (1010m), Sail Mhor, 3218ft (981m), Coire Mhic Fhearchair, and Liathach: Spidean a' Choire Leith, 3461ft (1054m), and Mullach an Rathain, 3356ft (1023m), Torridon

Date 29 June 1995 *Time* 9.40 a.m. *Camera* Fuji GX617 *Lens* SWD90mm f5.6

Two giant sentinels, Ruadh-stac Mor and Sail Mhor, appear to guard the entrance to Coire Mhic Fhearchair, a magnificent amphitheatre scalloped out of the Torridonian sandstone. This photograph was shot on the eve of the summer solstice, with the sun setting at its most northerly point.

pages 84–85 Lunga, Belnahua, Fladda, Luing and Seil islands, Sound of Luing, Argyll

Date 18 July 2000 *Time* 4.50 a.m. *Camera* Fuji GX617 *Lens* W180mm f6.7

Dawn over the Sound of Luing, with the Grey Dog below: the photograph was taken at high tide, just after slack water. Beyond Lunga, the islands of Belnahua, Fladda, Luing, Seil, Shuna and Torsa are collectively known as the Slate Islands.

page 86 Lichens on boulders, Lochan na h'Achalaise, Rannoch Moor

Date 22 September 2000 *Time* 9.50 a.m. *Camera* Arca Swiss F Metric 6 x 9 *Lens* Schneider Super-Angulon XL 90mm f5.6

Lochan na h'Achalaise provides continual opportunities for photography, as this image testifies. Among the elements of this timeless landscape that fascinate me are the rocks that have lain undisturbed on the waterline for centuries, and I was keen to capture their essence in this study.

page 87 Rocks and water, River Coupall, Glen Coe

Date 15 September 2000 *Time* 10.40 a.m. *Camera* Arca Swiss F Metric 6 x 9 *Lens* Schneider Apo-Symmar 210 f5.6

Often on location it proves impossible to pull together all the elements required to make a panoramic image work. At that stage I begin to look into the landscape for details, as was the case here. The image successfully captures the mood and feel of the place.

pages 88–89 A'Mhaighdean, 3173ft (967m), Beinn Lair, 2822ft (860m), and Fionn Loch from Beinn Airigh Charr, 2595ft (791m), Letterewe Forest

Date 22 July 2000 *Time* 9.20 p.m. *Camera* Fuji GX617 *Lens* W180mm f6.7

This was a memorable evening. The walk from Poolewe takes two hours before the mountain itself is climbed. Sharing the summit with some thirty wild goats, the views were spectacular. I set up on Beinn Airigh Charr as the sun's rays turned deep red.

pages 90–91 Beinn Alligin, 3235ft (986m), Liathach, 3356ft (1023m), and Beinn Damh, 2959ft (902m), Loch Shieldaig

Date 23 July 2000 *Time* 5.40 p.m. *Camera* Fuji GX617 *Lens* SWD90mm f5.6

The view east across Loch Shieldaig towards Beinn Alligin and Liathach was photographed in late afternoon. As dusk approached I returned, hoping to capture a big crimson sky, but shadow had covered the islands.

pages 92–93 Ben Nevis, 4409ft (1344m), Carn Mor Dearg arête beyond the Ring of Steall: An Gearanach, 3221ft (982m), An Garbhanach, 3198ft (975m), Am Bodach, 3386ft (1032m), Sgor an Lubhair, 3284ft (1001m), Sgurr a'Mhaim, 3606ft (1099m), Mamores, Lochaber

Date 22 August 2000 *Time* 9.20 p.m. *Camera* Fuji GX617 *Lens* SWD90mm f5.6

The dying sun illuminates the Carn Mor Dearg arête, with the north-east buttress of Ben Nevis already in shadow. Beyond lies the Ring of Steall, with An Gearananch and Sgurr a'Mhaim in sunlight, and the peaks of Glencoe.

pages 94–95 Loch Harpot and MacLeod's Tables: Healabhal Bheag, 1601ft (488m), and Healabhal Mhor, 1535ft (468m), Duirinish, Isle of Skye

Date 28 June 1995 *Time* 8.10 p.m. *Camera* Fuji GX617 *Lens* W180mm f6.7

From the summit of Bruach na Frithe, 3143ft (958m), these distinctive flat-topped hills can be seen in the distance. Like great natural altars, their name may be derived from *helgi fjall*, meaning 'holy fell'.

188

pages 96–97
Moonrise, Bla Bheinn (Blaven), 3045ft (928m) and Sgurr na Stri, 1631ft (497m), Cuillins, Isle of Skye

Date 5 July 1999 *Time* 9.10 p.m. *Camera* Fuji GX617 *Lens* W180mm f6.7

Considered one of the finest climbs in Skye, Blaven is the highest of the Cuillin outliers, linking the group to the Red Cuillin. Photographed from Marsco, 2415ft (736m) at sunset, the cloud forming was the onset of an inversion. Eigg and Rhum lie beyond.

AUTUMNAL EQUINOX TO WINTER SOLSTICE
(22–24 September to 21–22 December)

pages 102–103
Ring of Steall: An Gearanach, 3221ft (982m), An Garbhanach, 3198ft (975m), Am Bodach, 3386ft (1032m), from Sgor an Lubhair, 3284ft (1001m), Mamores, Lochaber

Date 27 September 2000 *Time* 9.00 p.m. *Camera* Fuji GX617 *Lens* W180mm f6.7

I set up the camera just as the sun dropped beneath the clouds and illuminated the summits of Am Bodach and Binnein Beag, 3094ft (940m), in a crimson light. I shot two rolls before the sun was lost.

pages 104–105
Clach Leathad, 3601ft (1098m), Meall a'Bhuiridh, 3635ft (1108m), Lochan na h'Achalaise, Rannoch Moor

Date 25 October 1997 *Time* 9.50 a.m. *Camera* Fuji GX617 *Lens* SWD90mm f5.6

Coire Ba, a tremendous corrie, lies on the far side of the sparkling lochan, whose surface is broken with boulders, reeds and bog-cotton. The morning was perfect for photography, with no wind to disturb the vibrant autumn foliage.

pages 106–107
Loch Beinn a'Mheadhoin, Fasnakyle Forest, Glen Affric

Date 16 October 1995 *Time* 8.20 a.m. *Camera* Fuji GX617 *Lens* SWD90mm f5.6

With remnants of the Old Caledonian Forest and native birch, Glen Affric is one of the finest glens in Scotland. Rising at dawn, I discovered a dense mist hanging above the water surface, creating a damp and eerie atmosphere, before the sun burned it off.

pages 108–109
Canisp, 2779ft (847m), Suilven, 2398ft (731m), Cul Mor, 2785ft (849m), Cul Beag, 2523ft (769m), and Stac Pollaidh, 2011ft (613m), Glencanisp, Sutherland

Date 10 October 1999 *Time* 9.50 a.m. *Camera* Fuji GX617 *Lens* SWD90mm f5.6

Glencanisp features one of the most spectacular landscapes in Scotland, including the 'island

mountains' of Suilven and Canisp, composed of Torridonian sandstone. I set up my camera during a squall, in anticipation of a rainbow.

pages 110–111
Sgurr nan Gillean, 3163ft (964m), from Marsco, 2415ft (736m), cloud inversion, Cuillins, Isle of Skye

Date 15 December 1995 *Time* 9.10 p.m. *Camera* Fuji GX617 *Lens* SWD90mm f5.6

The Cuillins are arguably the finest mountains in the British Isles; this magnificent peak commands a relatively isolated position at the end of the main ridge, accentuating its grandeur. The photograph was taken at sunset, as the sky turned crimson and yellow.

pages 112–113
Buachaille Etive Mor, 3353ft (1022m), and River Etive, Glen Etive

Date 15 December 1998 *Time* 9.50 a.m. *Camera* Fuji GX617 *Lens* SWD90mm f5.6

Without doubt one of the best known mountains in Scotland, commanding the gateway to Glencoe, this peak is a Mecca for walkers and climbers. I photographed it in the early morning across the River Etive, as I watched a mink quartering the riverbank.

page 114
Hoar frost and silver birch, River Merkland, Sutherland

Date 19 December 2000 *Time* 10.30 a.m. *Camera* Arca Swiss F Metric 6 x 9 *Lens* Schneider Super-Angulon XL 90mm f5.6

With an ambient temperature of 18°F (–8°C), a freezing fog blowing off Loch Merkland had covered the foliage along the river in a thick hoar frost. As the sun rose and burned off the mist the landscape assumed a quite surreal appearance.

page 115
Slioch, 3218ft (980m), Loch Maree, Letterewe Forest

Date 18 December 2000 *Time* 12.40 p.m. *Camera* Arca Swiss F Metric 6 x 9 *Lens* Schneider Apo-Symmar 210 f5.6 *Rating:* 5

Standing like a fortress, Slioch ('the Hill of Spears') stands between Torridon and the Great Wilderness – the Forests of Letterewe and Fisherfield. The low light was perfect, with no appreciable wind, and I used a telephoto to condense the elements.

pages 116–117
Sgurr Dubh, 2566ft (782m), Liathach: Spidean a'Choire Leith, 3461ft (1055m), and Beinn Eighe: Sgurr Ban, Coire Domhain, Glen Torridon

Date 19 December 1999 *Time* 8.50 a.m. *Camera* Fuji GX617 *Lens* W180mm f6.7

Highlighting its enormity of scale, Liathach rises in a single sweep from Upper Loch Torridon at sea level. As I photographed at dawn, a pink mist continually formed and dis-

persed above the snow-filled Coire Domhain on Beinn Eighe.

pages 118–119
Beinn Sgritheall, 3195ft (974m), Ladhar Bheinn, 3346ft (1020m), and Loch Hourn, Sound of Sleat, Isle of Skye

Date 15 December 1999 *Time* 10.40 a.m. *Camera* Fuji GX617 *Lens* W180mm f6.7

The view is south-east from Loch na Dal, across the Sound of Sleat and up Loch Hourn. To the east, the precipitous slopes of Beinn Sgritheall are seen: at the head of Loch Hourn stands Luinne Bheinn, 3081ft (939m) and to the east Ladhar Bheinn's summit ridge clears the clouds.

pages 120–121
River Abhainn Droma, Corrieshalloch Gorge, Braemore Forest

Date 18 December 1996 *Time* 10.20 a.m. *Camera* Fuji GX617 *Lens* SWD90mm f5.6

Towards the end of the ice age, as the ice cap melted, torrents of water scoured through solid rock, creating the long Gorge of Corrieshalloch. I was drawn to the ice patterns and the contrast between the solid and liquid states of the water.

pages 122–123
Stob Coire an Laoigh, 3661ft (1116m), Aonach Beag, 4049ft (1234m), Aonach Mor, 4006ft (1221m), and Ben Nevis, 4409ft (1344m), from Stob Choire Claurigh, 3862ft (1177m), Grey Corries, Lochaber

Date 18 December 1995 *Time* 4.00 p.m. *Camera* Fuji GX617 *Lens* W180mm f6.7

During an extended cold spell we climbed to the summit of Stob Choire Claurigh, which overlooks the Grey Corries and Ben Nevis. As the sun dropped, the views in every direction were breathtaking, as was the temperature, at –11°F (–24°C).

pages 124–125
The Cuillin Ridge from Glen Drynoch, Isle of Skye

Date 15 December 1999 *Time* 8.10 a.m. *Camera* Fuji GX617 *Lens* W180mm f6.7

At dawn, the pinks and lilacs of an overcast sky add drama to the Cuillin Ridge. To the east, Sgurr nan Gillean's triple ridges and the Basteir Tooth are visible. Sgurr a'Ghreadaidh, 3192ft (973m), lies centrally and further west is Sgurr Alasdair, 3255ft (992m).

pages 126–127
Garbh Bheinn, 2904ft (885m), Loch Linnie, Ardgour

Date 2 November 2000 *Time* 10.20 a.m. *Camera* Fuji GX617 *Lens* W180mm f6.7

Photographed from the confluence of Loch Leven and Loch Linnie, the distinctive mountains of the Ardgour dominate the view west. Locals refer to Garbh Bheinn as 'Queen Victoria's head', alleging a resemblance with the dead queen as she lay in state.

189

page 128 **Beinn Alligin: Tom na Gruagaich, 3025ft (922m), and Sgurr Mhor, 3235ft (986m), Upper Loch Torridon**

Date 19 December 1999 *Time* 10.30 a.m. *Camera* Arca Swiss F Metric 6 x 9 *Lens* Schneider Apo-Symmar 210 f5.6

Beinn Alligin is a beautifully sculpted mountain and can be seen to best advantage across Upper Loch Torridon, from just above the Torridon Hotel. Its two most distinctive features are the spectacular cleft of Eag Dhubh and Nan Rathanan, the Horns of Alligin.

page 129 **Derelict croft, Garve, Wester Ross**

Date 3 November 2000 *Time* 11.20 a.m. *Camera* Arca Swiss F Metric 6 x 9 *Lens* Schneider Super-Angulon XL 90mm f5.6

This croft with its corrugated roof would once have supported a family and some livestock. Fifty years on, it has become a symbol of a way of life which has passed forever. I was keen to show the croft in the context of its environment.

pages 130–131 **Loch an Eilein and Rothiemurchus Forest, Glen Feshie**

Date 27 October 1998 *Time* 8.50 a.m. *Camera* Fuji GX617 *Lens* SWD90mm f5.6

Across Loch an Eilein on the western flanks of Creag Fhiaclach, the treeline reaches 2133ft (650m), the highest in the Cairngorms. This image, shot at dawn, shows the autumn landscape at its best, before frosts begin to cut the leaves from the trees.

pages 132–133 **Pap of Glencoe, 2434ft (742m), Sgorr nam Fiannaidh, 3173ft (967m), Ballachulish, Loch Leven**

Date 2 November 2000 *Time* 10.10 a.m. *Camera* Fuji GX617 *Lens* W180mm f6.7

Sgorr na Ciche, more commonly known as the Pap of Glencoe, forms the western end of a long ridge which extends for 7 miles (11km) from the Devil's Staircase and over the Aonach Eagach. Bidean nam Bian, 3773ft (1150m), is visible to the south-east.

pages 134–135 **Beinn Fhada (Ben Attow), 3386ft (1032m), Saileag, 3136ft (956m), Sgurr a'Bhealaich Dheirg, 3399ft (1036m), Aonach Mheadhoin, 3284ft (1001m), Ciste Dhubh, 3212ft (979m), Glen Shiel, Kintail**

Date 14 December 1999 *Time* 9.20 a.m. *Camera* Fuji GX617 *Lens* SWD90mm f5.6

Extending 6 miles (9km) from east to west, Beinn Fhada is aptly named 'the Long Hill'. Photographed from Sgurr nan Spainteach, 3247ft (990m), at dawn, with the mountains of the North Shiel Ridge, the image captures the utter remoteness of the area.

pages 136–137 **Cul Mor, 2785ft (849m), Stac Pollaidh, 2011ft (613m), Cul Beag, 2523ft (769m), and Ben More Coigach, 2438ft (743m), Achnahaird Bay**

Date 14 December 1999 *Time* 10.40 a.m. *Camera* Fuji GX617 *Lens* W180mm f6.7

The confluence of mountain, moorland and seashore is always an interesting juxtaposition, particularly when the varied mountains of Inverpolly are included in the scene. Although they are relatively modest in height, the size and shape of these peaks make them striking subject-matter.

pages 138–139 **Stob Ghabhar, 3576ft (1090m), Loch Tulla, Inveroran, Argyll**

Date 17 December 1995 *Time* 8.50 a.m. *Camera* Fuji GX617 *Lens* SWD90mm f5.6

On a cold winter's morning at –8°F (–22°C) the sun climbed into the sky illuminating the deep sculpted corrie of Stob Ghabhar. The atmosphere was unusually dry, since all the available moisture was trapped in a solid state. A migrant flock of fieldfares chattered excitedly in the trees.

WINTER SOLSTICE TO VERNAL EQUINOX
(21–22 December to 20–21 March)

pages 144–145 **Ben Nevis, 4409ft (1344m), Coire na Ciste from Carn Mor Dearg, 4003ft (1220m), Lochaber**

Date 1 March 2000 *Time* 9.20 a.m. *Camera* Fuji GX617 *Lens* SWD90mm f5.6

Britain's highest mountain shares a common problem with many other big mountains – their most significant features face north-east. This means that it is almost impossible for them to be illuminated at sunrise in the months surrounding the winter solstice.

pages 146–147 **Moonrise, Lochan na h'Achalaise and Loch Ba, Rannoch Moor**

Date 19 February 2000 *Time* 5.50 p.m. *Camera* Fuji GX617 *Lens* W180mm f6.7

The view east across the Rannoch Moor shows the 'earth shadow' – the deep blue of the twilit wedge rises into red sky still lit directly by the sun. The juncture of blue shadow against red atmosphere looks far more splendid from high places.

pages 148–149 **Beinn Alligin, Sgurr Mhor, 3235ft (986m), and the Horns of Alligin from Tom na Gruagaich, 3025ft (922m), Torridon**

Date 10 January 2000 *Time* 3.30 p.m. *Camera* Fuji GX617 *Lens* SWD90mm f5.6

The last rays of sun illuminate Sgurr Mhor and Nan Rathanan. The conditions were near perfect, although the wind speed was stronger than I would have wished. Looking north-east, the snow-covered cliffs of A'Mhaighdean, 3173ft (967m) were visible.

pages 150–151 **Sgurr na Sgine, 3100ft (945m), the Saddle, 3314ft (1010m), and Five Sisters of Kintail: Sgurr na Ciste Duibhe, 3369ft (1027m), Sgurr Fhuaran, 3501ft (1067m), Glen Shiel, Kintail**

Date 6 January 1999 *Time* 9.20 a.m. *Camera* Fuji GX617 *Lens* SWD90mm f5.6

The photograph was shot from Sgurr nan Spainteach, 3247ft (990m), as the early mist dispersed. I had waited two years for the right season, weather and conditions to prevail. This image captures the essence of Kintail and is a personal favourite.

pages 152–153 **Suilven, 2398ft (731m), Canisp, 2779ft (847m), Cul Mor, 2785ft (849m), Loch Sionascaig from Stac Pollaidh, 2011ft (613m), Inverpolly Nature Reserve**

Date 7 February 1995 *Time* 9.50 a.m. *Camera* Fuji GX617 *Lens* SWD90mm f5.6

Suilven is the most westerly of the Assynt mountains and dominates the surrounding landscape. It has the remarkable ability to change shape dramatically when seen from different directions. I shot from the summit of Stac Pollaidh at dawn in February, the ultimate time.

pages 154–155 **Beinn an Dothaidh, 3294ft (1004m), Ben Dorain, 3530ft (1076m), Ben More, 3852ft (1174m), Stob Binnein, 3822ft (1165m), Cruach Ardrain, 3432ft (1046m), Beinn a'Chroin, 3084ft (940m), An Caisteal, 3264ft (995m), Beinn Chabhair, 3061ft (933m), from Stob Ghabhar, 3576ft (1090m), Argyll**

Date 19 February 2000 *Time* 5.10 p.m. *Camera* Fuji GX617 *Lens* W180mm f6.7

Taking advantage of an early snowfall, we made the ascent of Stob Ghabhar planning to shoot north over Glencoe. But as the sun set, the view south to Beinn Dorain and the Crianlarich Hills was superb – so much so that it made the front cover.

page 156 **The Cobbler (Ben Arthur), 2900ft (884m), Arrochar, Argyll**

Date 30 December 2000 *Time* 8.30 a.m. *Camera* Arca Swiss F Metric 6 x 9 *Lens* Schneider Apo-Symmar 210 f5.6

While the Cobbler does not qualify for Munro status, it assumes an almost Alpine stature when under snow. Although the mountain's location is close to Glasgow, it took me three years and six separate trips to achieve the necessary conditions.

page 157 Ben Lomond, 3195ft (974m), and Loch Lomond, Luss, Argyll

Date 30 December 2000 *Time* 3.40 p.m. *Camera* Arca Swiss F Metric 6 x 9 *Lens* Schneider Apo-Symmar 210 f5.6

Following two days of superb winter weather, the formation of cloud was the first sign of falling barometric pressure. Setting up the camera quickly, I captured the last rays of sun falling on the mountain before a comprehensive cloud base was established.

pages 158–159 An Teallach: Sgurr Fiona, 3478ft (1060m), Lord Berkley's Seat, 3379ft (1030m), and Corrag Bhuide, 3435ft (1047m), from Bidein a'Ghlas Thuill, 3484ft (1062m), Fisherfield Forest

Date 8 February 1995 *Time* 7.50 a.m. *Camera* Fuji GX617 *Lens* SWD90mm f5.6

I had planned this photograph for some time, making two unsuccessful attempts due to deteriorating weather. Setting out at 5 a.m. with head-torch and crampons, I reached the summit of Bidein a'Ghlas Thuill to witness a magnificent sunrise on Sgurr Fiona.

pages 160–161 St Cyrus Nature Reserve, Aberdeenshire

Date 10 February 1996 *Time* 7.40 a.m. *Camera* Fuji GX617 *Lens* SWD90mm f5.6

The sun rose into a clear sky, but at the same time a weather front approached from the west. This heightened the drama of the dawn and quickly snuffed out the sun. A skein of pink-footed geese flew overhead, followed by oystercatchers.

pages 162–163 Bidean nam Bian, 3773ft (1150m), Buachaille Etive Mor, 3353ft (1022m), Glen Etive from Stob Ghabhar, 3576ft (1090m), Argyll

Date 19 February 2000 *Time* 4.50 p.m. *Camera* Fuji GX617 *Lens* W180mm f6.7

Taken as the sun set over the peaks of Glencoe, this image is a distillation of the three best-known mountains in the Central Highlands: Bidean nam Bian in the west, Ben Nevis the highest point and Buachaille Etive Mor over to the east.

pages 164–165 Ben Lomond, 3195ft (974m), and Loch Lomond from Beinn Dubh, 2155ft (657m), Luss, Argyll

Date 29 December 1999 *Time* 9.10 a.m. *Camera* Fuji GX617 *Lens* W180mm f6.7

Dominating the view of Loch Lomond, Ben Lomond is a surprisingly difficult mountain to photograph. It is seen at its best from a point on Beinn Dubh above Luss. To achieve the image I had visualized, I needed an early snowfall around the winter solstice, and took the photograph at dawn.

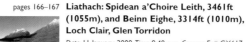

pages 166–167 Liathach: Spidean a'Choire Leith, 3461ft (1055m), and Beinn Eighe, 3314ft (1010m), Loch Clair, Glen Torridon

Date 11 January 2000 *Time* 9.40 a.m. *Camera* Fuji GX617 *Lens* SWD90mm f5.6

Photographed at dawn across Loch Clair, Liathach and Beinn Eighe are illuminated by a low winter sun. I waited until the sun was high enough to illuminate the stands of ancient Caledonian pines.

pages 168–169 Buachaille Etive Mor: Stob Dearg, 3353ft (1022m), River Etive, Glen Etive

Date 9 February 1995 *Time* 10.30 a.m. *Camera* Linhof 617S *Lens* Schneider Super-Angulon XL 90mm f5.6

Rising from Rannoch Moor, the Buachaille Etive Mor epitomizes mountain grandeur. Apart from Stob Dearg, its south-west ridge includes the tops of Stob na Doire, 3316ft (1011m), Stob Coire Altrium, 3086ft (941m), and Stob na Broige, 3136ft (956m).

page 170 Rock and ice, River Etive, Glen Etive

Date 28 December 1999 *Time* 11.30 a.m. *Camera* Linhof Technikardan 5 x 4 *Lens* Schneider Super-Angulon XL 90mm f5.6

Standing amongst these giant boulders, shaped and smoothed over centuries by running water, I experienced some sort of affinity with the natural world – an appreciation that goes beyond words, precisely the quality that a powerful photograph should distil.

page 171 Buachaille Etive Mor: Stob Dearg, 3353ft (1022m), River Etive, Glen Etive

Date 28 December 1999 *Time* 9.50 a.m. *Camera* Linhof Technikardan 5 x 4 *Lens* Schneider Super-Angulon XL 90mm f5.6

Epitomizing the height of experience in Scottish mountaineering, the Buachaille Etive Mor is a symbol for superlatives. Photographed here at dawn in clearing mist, it is one of the few mountains that are sufficiently distinctive to be instantly recognizable.

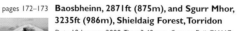

pages 172–173 Baosbheinn, 2871ft (875m), and Sgurr Mhor, 3235ft (986m), Shieldaig Forest, Torridon

Date 10 January 2000 *Time* 3.40 p.m. *Camera* Fuji GX617 *Lens* W180mm f6.7

Alpenglow bathes the summit of Sgurr Mhor and Eag Dhubh, the great slash. Beyond, Baosbheinn's summit ridge glows in the red light. These conditions had been elusive and took me three years to record.

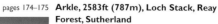

pages 174–175 Arkle, 2583ft (787m), Loch Stack, Reay Forest, Sutherland

Date 13 January 2000 *Time* 10.30 a.m. *Camera* Fuji GX617 *Lens* SWD90mm f5.6

Stretching 2 miles (3km) along the northern shore of Loch Stack. Arkle is a distinctive mountain. To the north-west a magnificent amphitheatre of stepped corries and lochans are formed with the southern end of Foinaven, 2989ft (911m).

pages 176–177 Stob Coire Easain, 3658ft (1115m), Stob a'Choire Mheadhion, 3625ft (1105m), beyond Geal Charn, 3442ft (1049m), Beinn a'Chlachair, 3566ft (1087m), Beinn Eibhinn, 3615ft (1102m), Aonach Beag, 3661ft (1116m), Geal-charn, 3714ft (1132m), Ben Alder, 3766ft (1148m), Schiehallion, 3553ft (1083m), from Stob Choire Claurigh, 3862ft (1177m), Grey Corries, Lochaber

Date 28 December 1995 *Time* 3.40 p.m. *Camera* Fuji GX617 *Lens* W180mm f6.7

On a late winter's evening alpenglow illuminates the high glaciated plateau, which includes the remote peaks of Ben Alder and Beinn Bheoil, 3343ft (1019m). When the sun disappeared, the temperature dropped rapidly as we began the long walk home.

pages 178–179 Sgurr a'Bhealaich Dheirg, 3399ft (1036m), Aonach Mheadhoin, 3284ft (1001m), Ciste Dhubh, 3212ft (975m), Loch Cluanie, Glen Shiel

Date 17 March 1997 *Time* 11.10 a.m. *Camera* Linhof 617S *Lens* Schneider Super-Angulon 90mm f5.6

This was one of those remarkable moments when the air is completely still. The mountains of the North Shiel Ridge beyond Loch Cluanie are perfectly reflected in the water. Within five minutes the wind had returned and the water surface rippled.

pages 180–181 The mountains of Lochaber from Stob Choire Claurigh, 3862ft (1177m), Grey Corries, Lochaber

Date 28 December 1995 *Time* 3.20 p.m. *Camera* Fuji GX617 *Lens* SWD90mm f5.6

The vista from the peak is spectacular and I set up my camera as the setting sun was making the transition from yellow to red. In every direction, all I could see through the viewfinder was snow-covered mountains.

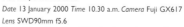

ACKNOWLEDGEMENTS

I would like to thank Geraldine, my wife, for her patience and understanding during the years I worked on this book. Also my daughter Alexandra and my son Laurence, who selflessly accepted that I couldn't always be there. In Scotland, climatic conditions change quickly and the need to react to a stable weather period is essential. Trips planned at short notice left many family and social engagements in turmoil.

Those involved in stressful endeavour acknowledge the importance of equipment and advice and I would like to thank the management of Tiso for their support and encouragement during this project.

The images themselves would not exist without the technology on which I depend, and I would like to acknowledge Fuji Photo Film (UK) Ltd for their cameras and film, Hasselblad (UK) Ltd, Canon UK Ltd and Robert White Photographic.

Finally, thanks to Peter Duncan and Nova Jayne Heath of Constable & Robinson, whose enthusiasm and vision for the project was a constant source of encouragement.

For further information regarding prints, posters and calendars published by Colin Prior, visit the on-line store at www.earthgallery.net. A range of panoramic prints is available, together with regular updates that will keep you informed on Colin's work on new projects.

SCOTS PINE AND BIRCH, NEVIS GORGE, GLEN NEVIS